Salon.com

SALON.COM
Copyright © Artpower International Publishing Co., Ltd.

CARTPOWER™

Designer: Allen Hong
Chief Editor: Emily Luo

Address: 21/F, Skyline Commercial Center, 71~77 Wing
        Lok Street, SheungWan, Hong Kong

Tel: 852 3184 0676
Fax: 852 2543 2396
URL: www.artpower.com.cn
E~mail: artpower@artpower.com.cn

ISBN 978-988-15742-9-9

Printed in China

Preface

Giulio Patrizi

In what direction moves the contemporary architecture and interior design? Can you predict the future? Who are the creative forms that shape and leave their traces in our time, or more importantly open up new possibilities?

It is very difficult to express a critical opinion on the creativity of their time. The most admired artistic innovations are usually the result of previous eras and phases. Looking ahead means to deduce what are the guides that shape the art of planning and design.

In a creative world where more and more globalization from New York to Hong Kong, from Rome to Beijing is being built in the same way, designers play an important role to emphasize the origin and design of the place: a sort of identity of belonging, where each of us, albeit in a comprehensive manner, apply them their knowledge and their background, thereby creating his own style: a mix of culture, awareness, design, and methodology.

This book will present an overview of projects related to the internal world of beauty and wellness, such as barbershop, salon, etc. around the world.

Increasingly, large employers are turning to the most creative designers to design their homes, their shops, their showrooms in various world capitals, a sign of a philosophy of a modern communication and patronage, which makes it possible to experience in this field.

Contents

BARTEK JANUSZ HAIRDRESSER

Location: Warszawa, Poland   Client: Bartek Janusz

MooMoo — Founded in 2008 by Jakub Majewski and Lukasz Pastuszka. In 2009 Wallpaper* Magazine selected MOOMOO as one of the best 30 young offices in the world. Our works has been previously shown on exhibitions in London, Shanghai, Rotterdam and Brussels.

 Project Information

Design of the place is based around a simple concept derived from the jagged, angular forms created by free falling hair which can be found on the floor of any busy salon. This striking arrangement which occurs on the floor will now be transformed throughout the interior to create a dynamic, vibrant space. The salon carries a secondary function - it also serves as an exhibition space for the work of young designer's, the clothes hand picked by a famous Polish designer Gosia Baczynska. A fitting room is concealed behind the curtain wall which visually separates the retail function from the hair dresser's zone. Inclined wall planes are bisected by horizontal cuts which open shelf space for the exhibited hair products along with the functional sink surface. Tall slender mirror columns serve to both clients and the stylists, offering abundance of storage and function inside. Spacial dynamism and multiple reflections offer multiple perspectives into the space resulting in a playful, creative environment for the hair masters. Waiting space is strategically located along the window openings as well as at the entrance to offer a unique viewing experience for customers.

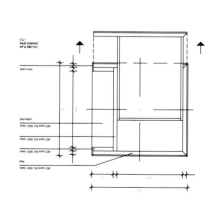

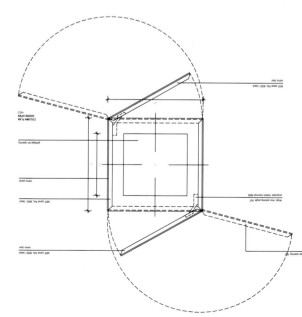

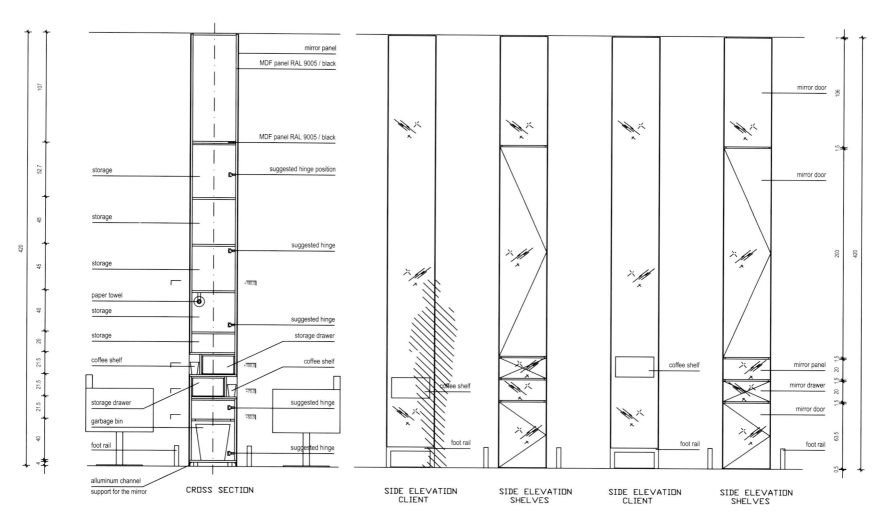

CROSS SECTION

mirror panel
MDF panel RAL 9005 / black
MDF panel RAL 9005 / black
suggested hinge position
storage
storage
suggested hinge
storage
paper towel
suggested hinge
storage
storage
storage drawer
coffee shelf
coffee shelf
storage drawer
suggested hinge
garbage bin
foot rail
suggested hinge
alluminum channel
support for the mirror

SIDE ELEVATION CLIENT

coffee shelf
foot rail

SIDE ELEVATION SHELVES

coffee shelf
foot rail

SIDE ELEVATION CLIENT

coffee shelf
foot rail

SIDE ELEVATION SHELVES

mirror door
mirror door
mirror panel
mirror drawer
mirror door
foot rail

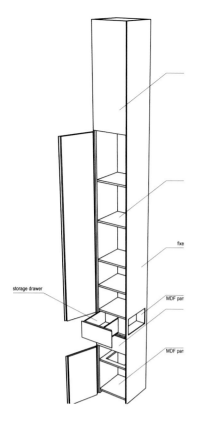

storage drawer

fixe

MDF pan

MDF pan

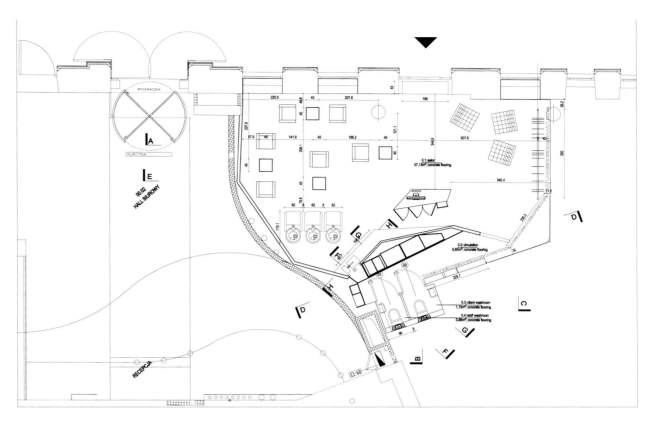

BRILLIAGE

Design: GLAMOROUS co.,ltd.   Client: Vierge   Photography: ©Nacasa & Partners Inc

Yasumichi
Morita

Born in Osaka, Japan in 1967. Starting with the project at China Hong-Kong in 2001, his work is successfully and globally expending to the cities including New York, London and Shanghai. His creative activities have expanded into graphic and product design beyond his original career in interior design. Prize: THE LONDON LIFESTYLE AWARDS (AQUA LONDON), The Andrew Martin Interior Designers of the Year Awards etc…

Project Information

The design theme is "Sparkling air bubbles in the water".
The sunlight coming through the surface of the water is reflected by the air bubbles and gives more brilliance to the world.
Silence, clear world in the water is a completely different world. Guests will discover and come into another world, as if they become a mermaid.

The clearness and the cleanness of the space are very remarkable on the cut booth. Numerous round studs are placed on the panel screen of stainless mirror finishing on back of the cut booth. These round studs like air bubbles floating in the water, are also reflected several times by other screen panel of stainless mirror finishing on opposite side exterior, and the fantastic atmosphere is produced with the endless reflections.

Going through the waiting space where the samples are displayed in niche showcase placed on the wall in black colored stainless steel, guests will reach to the nail salon. Glass walls painted in several different beiges compose a harmony of elegant gradation in monotone. In contrast with the cut booth, the sharp lines of the design motives unify this space in simple modern. Style and provide a relaxing and peaceful mood. The lighting fixtures made of clashed glass, designed originally by Mr. Takahiro Kondo, are symbolically twinkled in this space.

1
9
8
0

Shiro

Art Director: 1980 / Hiromasa Mori   Client: aPreko   Photography: 1980

Hiromasa Mori
Takuya Hosokai

1980 was founded by Hiromasa Mori and Takuya Hosokai in Japan, 2005. They have worked on several architectural projects for over two years and have two realized projects, Kuro and Shiro, which were built in Fukui, Japan. The main themes of 1980's work were primarily in the division between internal and external space, and the use of non-physical cues to separate space.

Currently Hiromasa is a co-founder of HYAD and is based in Japan, and Takuya is a founder of TAKUYAHOSOKAI and is based in Madrid.

waiting space +150

car park

cut space +150

UP

cut space

-50

shampoo space +150

massage space +150

1 FL PLAN 1/100

N

cut space +2,600

UP

shampoo space +2,600

Japanese room +2,650

2FL PLAN 1/100

closet +4,650

Japanese room +5,650

UP

terrace

staff room +5,200

UP

meeting room +5,200

+5,400

3FL PLAN 1/100

1 FL_plan diagram

2FL_plan diagram

3FL_plan diagram

section_A diagram

section_B diagram

■ core
□ void
---- Z axis virtual boundary
---- X,Y,Z axis virtual boundary

japanese room +5,650

closet +4,650

cut space +2,600

cut space +150

reception +150

waiting space +150

Section 1/100

meeting room +5200

Japanese room +5,650

cut space +2,600

shampoo space +150

reception +150

Section 1/100

Company	1980
Typology / Purpose	Beauty salon
Site area	194.26 m²
Architectural area	78.17 m²
Total floor area	166.79 m²
Number of stories	3
Structure	Steel construction

Project Information

Shiro is a beauty salon in Japan.

Unlike a typical approach to beauty salon design, the design did not begin with the concept of ensuring "every space is connected on one floor".
Instead, this building is designed to "connect and divide using virtual separations in 3 dimensions".

These virtual separations are created in 3 dimensions using a combination of open space and solid volumes. A number of voids in the floor also create non-physical barriers as a means of separating spaces.

Whilst the initial entrance, the waiting space is 4m in height; the 1st floor "shampoo space" is just 2.3m high and a second shampoo space on the 2nd floor with a height of 2.5m. In contrast with the cut, void spaces vary from 7.5m on the 1st floor, to a 2.9m cut space on the 2nd floor. These big voids, cut between each volume, produce a dynamic and extraordinary space with a great variety in spatial qualities as a client progresses through the building, and continues their beauty treatment.

The design also wish to encourage the introduction of a large quantity of foliage in this space, a method of introducing a sense of seasonal variation and providing a connection with the outside environment.

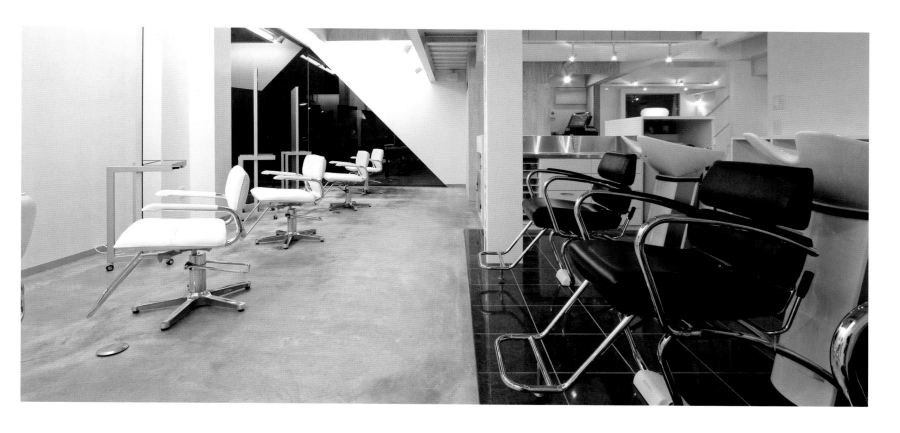

Salon of Wind & Water

Daniel Tiong
Allen Chen

Daniel Tiong & Allen Chen are Interior Designers in Singapore who tries to elevating interior spaces into more than one can imagine. They are design trained and capable in Retail, Commercial, Residential, Office, Public Space, Furniture Design and etc.

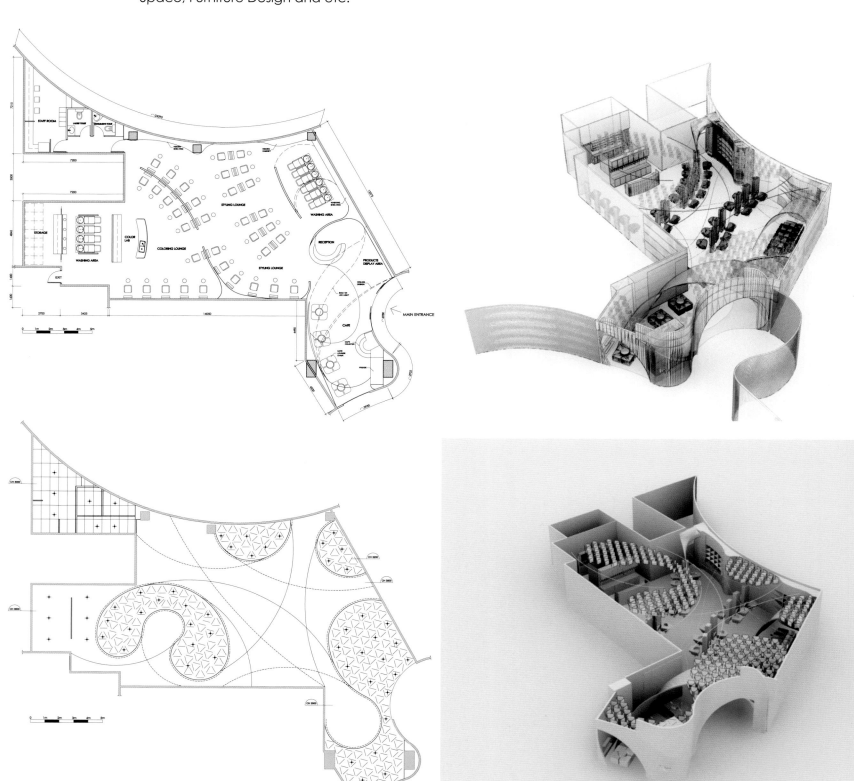

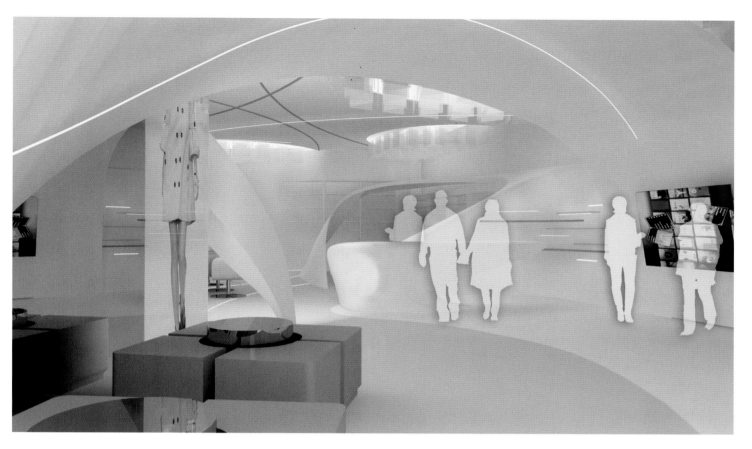

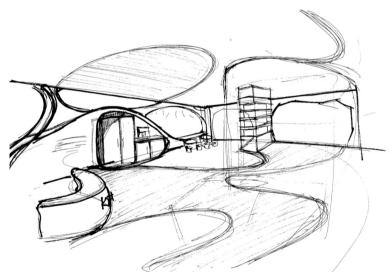

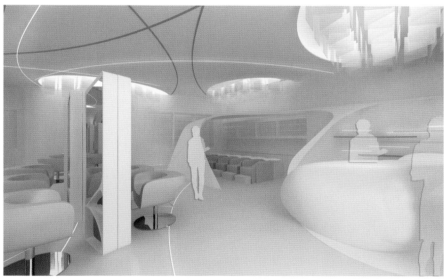

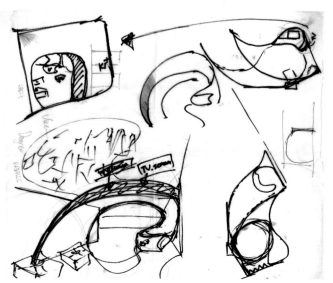

Project Information

The design of the salon was inspired by "Wind & Water". The inspirations come from the energetic of Wind and tranquil of water which commonly appears in any Salon. The designs translate nature energetic movement of wind and the unique tranquil patterns of water into the interior space; foresee a futuristic yet organic interior atmosphere.

The Interior lines and LED light strips which appear on the ceiling and flooring present the energetic moves of wind. The present of interior structure, furniture and fittings are in organic forms which observe from water patterns and its behavior. Translucent membrane features hanging from the ceiling that once the wind blow passing by the features will create gentle movement which bring the ceiling "alive" and yet activate human imagination. It may look like clouds or something abstract, but yet it brings interior space more fun.

Simply shades of black, cool grey and white on the wall, ceiling, flooring and furniture balance the brightness of lighting; neatly present the layout of the space. Spotless and calm ambience merges with smooth and curvy interior structure, create a different experience of new Salon interior.

GAMMASTORE by GAMMA

GAMMA &amp GAMMA &amp officially born 30 years ago. The design team makes an expert fusion of design and production techniques, together with the historical knowledge of the profession with its own specific needs. Quality of construction as well as salon image are the key elements upon which GAMMA &amp and BROSS SPA focuses its entrepreneurial commitment. Now the company sells its upscale furniture in more than 50 countries and the distribution network has been developed in more than 30 countries.

Project Information

If it is true that the cultural value of design is to make it available to everyone, then GAMMASTORE is the ultimate expression. Expensive industrial production that was available to the few affluent in the past, today is reality for everyone. With GAMMASTORE it is possible to have products at extraordinary costs which is timeless and modern, integrating beauty and function, with materials that accent the essential clean lines. Design is the added value that makes the difference and it is obvious. A pulsating live design coming out of the museum and into everyday life is valued for what it is and not what it costs. Accessible luxury has arrived: it's called GAMMASTORE.

ECO CHIC (GammaStore Collection):

Welcome to the world of sustainable development, with a life style that use the recyclable materials; where products are made in an eco-compatible environment, with technology and manufacturing processes that use adult qualified and approved labor. Ethics and esthetics finally come together where form and material converge to give a deep sense and awareness to profound values.

FORMAL CHIC (GammaStore Collection):

It's the trendy salon yet formal and elegant. It picks the most innovative and interesting fashion elements to create a timeless classic.

LIGHT PERFORMANCE (GammaStore Collection):

Illuminated volumes animate the salon during the day and projects an image on the street at night.
The light becomes a dominant element creating space with its weightless effect. It is a concept dedicated to those who
desire a style that before its time and lasts. "Light Performance" as time and space converge toward the infinite.

BLACK PORSCHE by F.A.Porsche (MG BROSS Collection):

Many things seem truly impossible until the opposite is demostrated, with courage, creativity and intuition. Only in this way we can transcend the limits, only in this way we can attain what has never been accomplished before. Driven by the constant quest for innovation, those who seek the impossible obtain the possible.
This has led us to create a new salon furniture range conceived by F.A. PORSCHE, the world's leading designers. "TSU CHAIR": a projected dream, an idea that seemed unattainable, until today.

Jigsaw

Location: Nigata, Japan   Design Agency: Future-scape Architects   Client: owner of beauty salon

Daigo Ishii

Daigo Ishii + Future-scape Architects was founded in 1999. We design interior, architecture and urban design, considering the relation with place and environment. The place is a basis of the identity of people and the architecture connects the identity with people. In concrete terms, the key word is " Continuous and Independent". The architecture is designed in consideration with the continuity with the townscape or landscape and, at the same time, with delicate difference that offers the slight independence from the surroundings.

1st Floor Plan 1/100

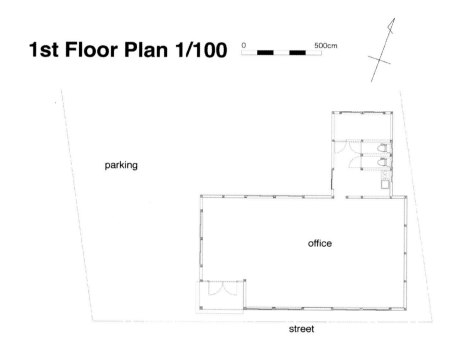

before the renovation

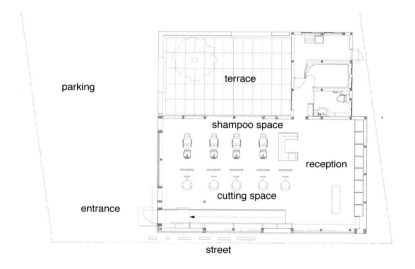

after the renovation

 Project Information

This is a renovation work of an old-fashioned wooden office. It was a mediocre architecture, but the designers appreciated the time of 25 years when it existed at the same place. The designer re-designed it expressing the respect to the existing state but creating the new possibility. The succession of the memory also connected with sustainability. The windows on the exterior wall were scattered based on the principal related to this architecture. The horizontal position was the same as the existing position. Meanwhile the vertical position was based on the height peculiar to the architecture. It was not a random design but related to the rule of the existing architecture. It didn't break the rhythm of townscape maintained for long time but improve it.

In the interior, the mirror indispensable for the beauty salon was used as an apparatus of architecture. Besides, the floor and the ceiling were also finished in gloss paint that reflected the light and the scenery.

The synergy effect that the mirrors produced with the windows on the outside wall made complicated the simple interior space. As the time passed, the state of the natural light or the weather changed, and, as a result, according to the reflection of the mirror or high gloss paint, the impression of the interior also changed. The impression of the interior was always different and the atmosphere of the outdoor and the comfort of the outdoor was brought into the interior.

window position of exisiting architecture
window position in the horizontal direction

before renovation

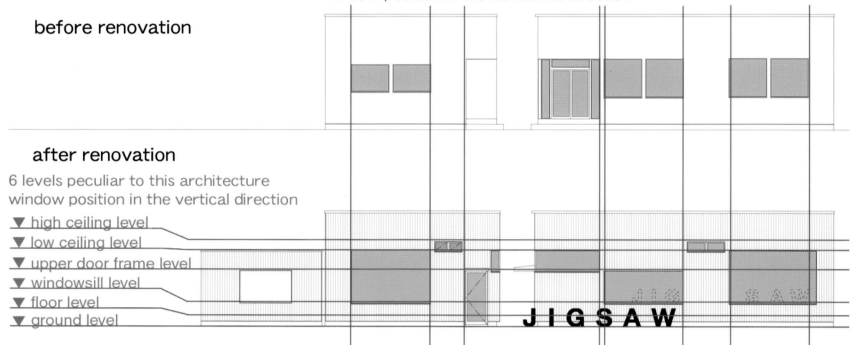

after renovation

6 levels peculiar to this architecture
window position in the vertical direction

▼ high ceiling level
▼ low ceiling level
▼ upper door frame level
▼ windowsill level
▼ floor level
▼ ground level

JIGSAW

Hairstyling Nafi

Design Agency: SÜDQUAI patente.unikate. in collaboration with ZMIK   Client: Hairstyling Nafi, Basel   Photography: Eik Frenzel

SÜDQUAI patente. unikate. in collaboration with ZMIK

SÜDQUAI patente unikate was founded by Katharina Widmer and Matteo Winkler – an artist and a loving couple.

The two artists combine the most differing media in order to create new and unique resolutions.

In the era of digital manufacturing technology they appreciate the aesthetics of the analogue, the handmade and the irrational.

They set a high value on quality instead of quantity and wish to slow down in the fast moving time.

They are interested in the process within their work. They regard their work as part of their life and their life as part of their work. Stereotype ways of thinking and designing bore them. They don't like any constraints and they love freedom.

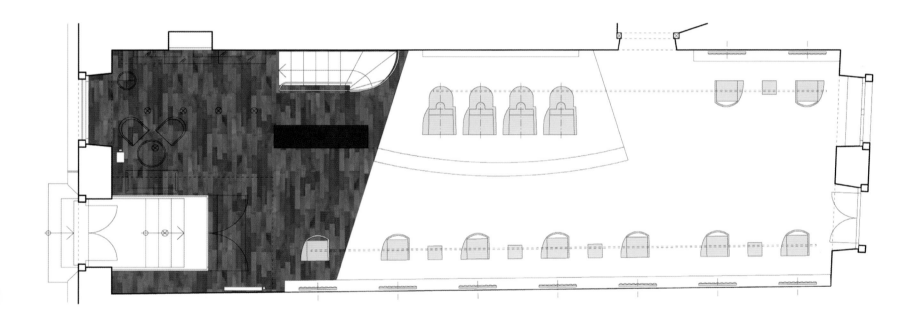

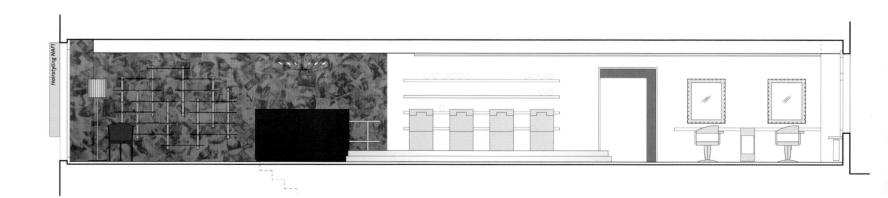

 Project Information

The hairdresser Hairstyling Nafi in Basel's historic city centre has undergone a reconstruction. The space is now subdivided into two zones, which are being separated by a sharp border. The two areas strongly contrast in their function as well as in their spatial atmosphere. The ceiling and the walls of the reception zone are entirely covered with vintage cuttings from Vogue, photocopied onto packaging paper. Opulently furnished and bathed in warm light, the reception is an invitation for a rest, for purchasing products and for discussing the newest styling trends. The white studio, however, is the absolute antithesis. Here nothing distracts the work of the hair stylist. The ideal light for working, the bright and glossy surfaces and the minimal, metallic furnishings put the newly cut hairstyles into the centre of attention. The customer – literally being framed by the mirror – brings the room alive with the reflection of his face.

Jenny House

Location: KangNam District, Seoul, Korea   Design Agency: DI CESARE DESIGN

ANDREA DI CESARE
LUCA DI CESARE

Based in Milan since 2001, DI CESARE DESIGN is present also in Shanghai (China) and Seoul (Korea), designing concept stores, concept hotels and restoration spaces, interactive urban installations as well as living interiors.

We offer a special know-how in the development of brand identity and retail design projects for the fashion and luxury brands who need to create an excellent corporate image to ensure a high perceived quality.

DI CESARE DESIGN is formed by talented individuals working in different fields and everyone moved by a holistic and excellent sense of project. Interior decoration, architecture, landscape art, industrial design, visual merchandising, graphic and communication are all the disciplines we mix to offer a full development of the concepts we devise for our customers.

Jenny House is a VIP luxury beauty salon sited in Seoul, Korea. This is the restyle of the first shop (there are three in all).

The location is in the heart of the VIP district of CheongDam (GangNam Gu), next to the most famous fashion shops.

The beauty salon is developed on two floors with an additional floor for the offices and the terrace on the roof, for private parties and special events.

The third floor is mostly dedicated to the wedding services (hair styling, make-up, dressing room, meeting room); the forth floor is dedicated to the standard services (hair styling, nail design, head and foot spa). Each floor has a huge space for waiting and enjoying a drink while watching television or reading magazines.

The concept is based on the myth of Narcisus, the legendary guy whose beauty was acknowledged everywhere in the ancient Greece.

The legend tells about Narcisus as a beautiful guy loved by every girl, even by the nymphs who used to live in the fairy forest. Narcisus used to look at himself reflected on the water of the lake.

Here starts our story; a beautiful face built by mdf panels laser-cut. The face is reflected on the opposite black mirror, like a dark water pool in the forest. And all around is the forest that the designers recreated with organic shapes that hold the mirrors. And a big waving tree in the middle that is functionally used as a sitting area.

The white, smooth shaped metal ribbons, the reflections on mirrors; the general atmosphere is the one of a wonderland.

On the third floor, the space dedicated to wedding, the white and the pink recreate the pure environment that welcome the bride. A 10 meters long wall is decorated with a double layer of laser-cut metal panel that interact with light giving always a moving impression.

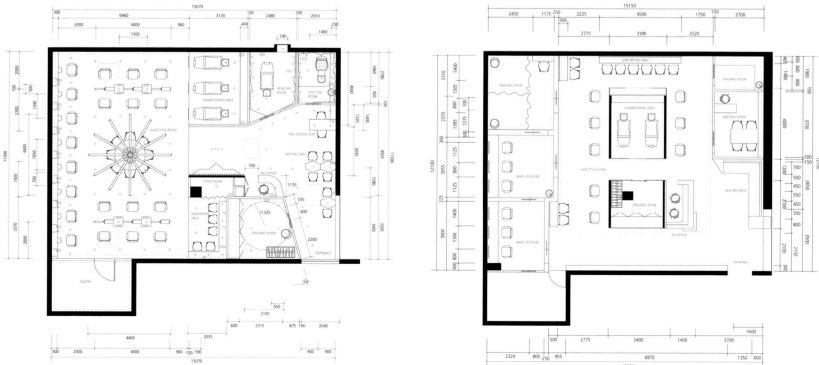

EARTH

Design Agency: ICHIRO NISHIWAKI DESIGN OFFICE INC.   Client: EARTH HOLDINGS INCORPORATED   Photography: Nacasa&Partners Inc.

ICHIRO
NISHIWAKI

Born in Tokyo, Japan.
Worked as interior designer at IIJIMA DESIGN after graduating from Kuwasawa Design School.
In 1991, founded ICHIRO NISHIWAKI DESIGN OFFICE INC.
In 1997, founded N-Planning.
Sevral prize of "JCD design Award" and "NASHOP Lighting Awards" etc.
Design policy "not only make the client pleased by producing shop,but also
make the shop doing good business", always consider about the shop after building.

Project Information

This is a dual-level shop with an inside staircase installed by design from construction. As there are rows of all kinds of shops trade in the neighborhood, a plan with a maximally open frontage rather than the building design was made the given condition, keeping in mind to expose the internal space to the outside. To this end, efforts were made to facilitate lead-in to the second level by placing the styling stations in the rear and installing a staircase near the entrance. The wellhole that is formed inevitably was made the point of the interior framework of the project. Inside the walls supporting the staircase are VIP booths, and the surface layer of the outer wall was covered over with a photograph of rose flowers. The CI of the EARTH brand was enlarged to a giant size and printed on glossy paper.

Each station was partitioned by string curtains to secure privacy from the next station without a sense of closure, and their series was adopted as a framework of design. The entirety was coordinated in fresh and neat white. Wallpapers with luxuriousness were selected as accents to produce a coexistence of fine quality and brilliance.

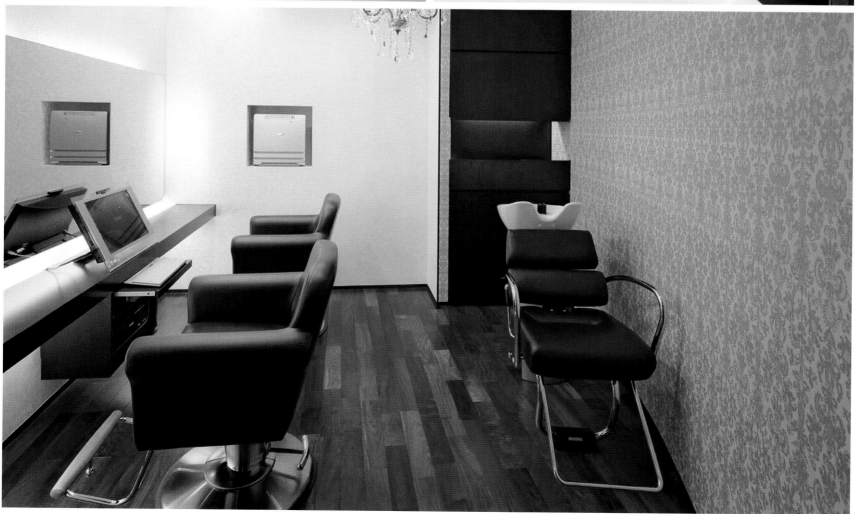

Hooker & Young

Franchisee: Lesley Charles   Client: Hooker & Young   Budget: £100,000

Gary Hooker & Michael Young

Gary Hooker and Michael Young are both in HJ's British Hairdressing Awards Hall of Fame for their individual achievements in winning the Northern and North Eastern categories three times respectively. Being nominated for British was an ambition they have had for many years.

"After entering the Hall of Fame, British was next on our list. We have been consistent players in the industry for almost 30 years and are committed to raising the standards."

In fact, they are constantly raising the standards at shows and shoots, recreating looks that are glamorous and luxurious, contemporary with an edge. "Being nominated as a couple is our biggest achievement, as is building our recognised and respected brand with a great team."

Having a great team is one aspect the dynamic duo love about their job, along with seeing people grow, travelling and meeting new people. The past 12 months have been a whirlwind for the pair, but while life has never been busier, they wouldn't change a thing.

"Life is crazy, manic, stressful and exciting. We are really focused on the brand and opened two more salons this year, with our first franchise. We hope to move more into this direction in the future."

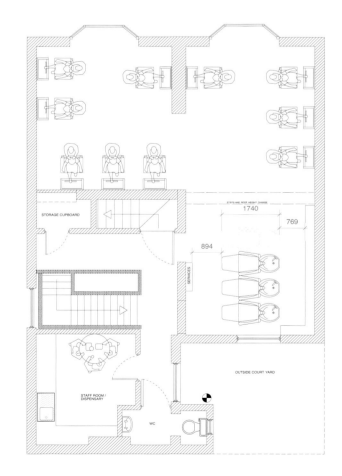

Offering a retail experience like no other, this salon brings a new level of hairdressing to the Darlington area. Set in the stylish Grange Road, this townhouse salon is a haven of tranquility.

The salon oozes opulence, from the Swarovski crystals hanging in the hair spa to the flocked metallic wallpaper used throughout the building.

The backwash hair spa is one of the main features of the salon, with three celebrity backwashes which convert into beds and massage. Other stand-out features include the wall of mirrors in the lounge, the chandelier on the staircase and two beautiful bay windows in the salon.

KAZE MOOCA

Location: Rua Paes de Barros, 2712, Mooca, São Paulo, Brazil   Client: Haruo Ishii   Structural Design: Companhia de Projetos

FGMF arquitetos

Founded in 1999, Forte, Gimenes & Marcondes Ferraz (FGMF) has shown in these few years the ability and flexibility to deal with a wide range of design types and scales.

Based on the partners' international and academic experience, the studio pursues a different and fresh approach to every design proposed. There are no pre-determined formulae or strict method defined – we start always from scratch and make the design process our research tool for a brand new vision of the city.

We are proud to have earned several relevant national architectural prizes, mostly awarded by the Brazilian Institute of Architects (IAB-SP). Such prizes stimulate our passion and focus on creative and efficient designs.

Project Information

The two-storey building benefits from constant natural lighting, and has an efficient natural cooling system.

Facing north (equivalent to south in the northern hemisphere), the facade has permanent contribution of the hot brazilian sun. The building is then "dressed" in a continuous steel crating to provides shade to a linnear garden that separates the crating and the glass curtain in the two floors. Sucked inside, this plant-cooled air then avoids the need of air conditioning.

Cor-ten steel structure has only one pair of pillars on the suspended part body, freeing space for the parking undergroud. The struture takes advantage of the building's geometry to provide a 9-meter-long cantilever at the edge.

Hairu Hair Treatment

Design Agency: CHRYSTALLINE ARTCHITECT   Photography: William Sebastian

Christophorus Jauhari

Born at Jakarta, Indonesia on 1983, Chris graduated in 2005 from Tarumanagara University as a valedictorian with a perfect grade on his final assignment entitled "Garbage Recycling Station" in which his professors called as a "novelty and extraordinary" concept.

After his study, he assigned himself as a freelance architect for 2 years, searching for in-depth experience, before finally establishing his own architecture firm in 2007 named, "Chrystalline Artchitect".

To him, architecture is an inexplicable form of art, which can't be categorized as abstract, "I believe there is no such thing called abstract. There is always a hidden sequence within the way it's arranged. That's one of the things I obtain from practice in architecture."

His passion for architecture has never stopped growing. His fervor expands even more, especially when it comes to working with insubstantial conditions, "For me, more obstacles emit even more unexpected, exceptional designs. Working under intense circumstances enables my inner creativity to outburst rapidly."

Chris explained that his inspiration mostly comes from nature-form sources, "I try to create a functional space, with clean, and detail touches of Mother Nature interpretation. I prefer to use the actual,

earthy color of the materials itself. It appeals more natural, moreover, it is easier to maintain, with longer sustainability." Chris remarked, "Meticulous details are also a necessity and interesting to explore with. Those detailed attributes fascinate me in every way."

His scope of work includes mostly residential, hospitality, institutional, and retail stores. His extraordinary designs have led him to be the Finalist of Building of the Year 2010 award by Archdaily and to receive special recognition from "Bravacasa" Indonesia magazine for best design in lightning, dining room and bedroom.

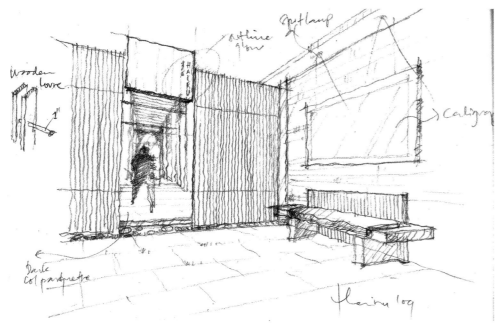

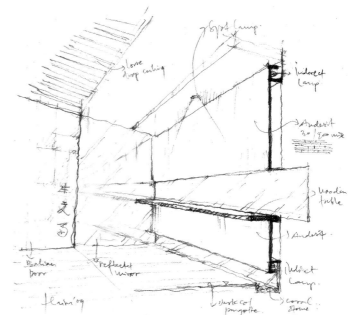

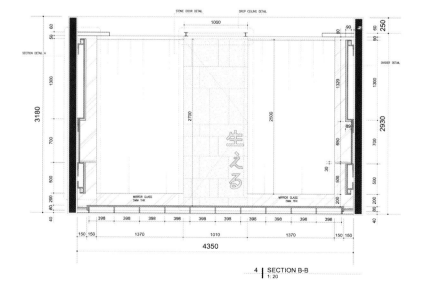

4 | SECTION B-B
1: 20

Project Information

Started with modular design and build through generous clean and simple detail, perform in natural material scheme and color, brought you to the difference experience of leisure. It may looks like a salon, but Hairu is a hair health-care, such as treatment for losing hair, hair spa & massage.

The vocal point is the two faced rough bali-an stone which also as a transition door to the wash area. The ribbon mirror on the both side wall is carried through the view of all the space with the private sight just for the client without having eyes contact with the therapist.

The soft material, vitrage, is acting as a divider which I could be moved to get along with the other. And the hard material, cotton, is as a permanent divider from the main corridor.

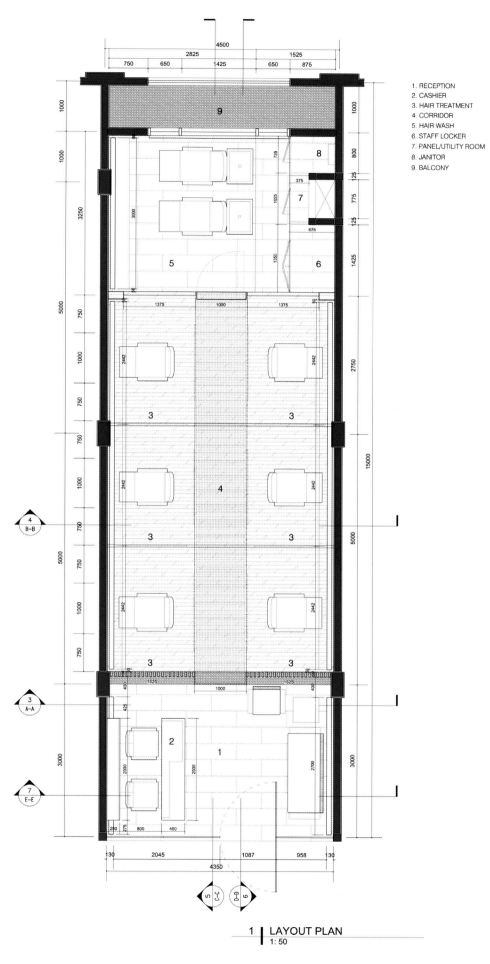

1. RECEPTION
2. CASHIER
3. HAIR TREATMENT
4. CORRIDOR
5. HAIR WASH
6. STAFF LOCKER
7. PANEL/UTILITY ROOM
8. JANITOR
9. BALCONY

1 | LAYOUT PLAN
1 : 50

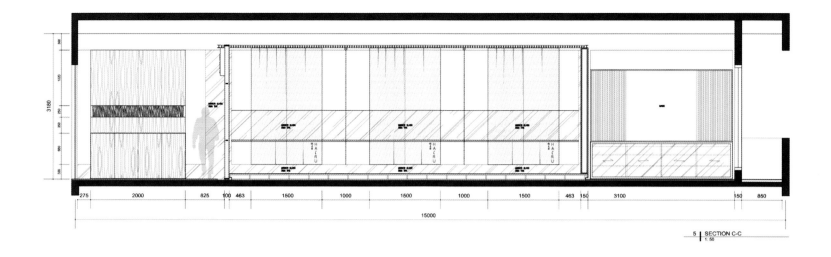

5 | SECTION C-C
1:50

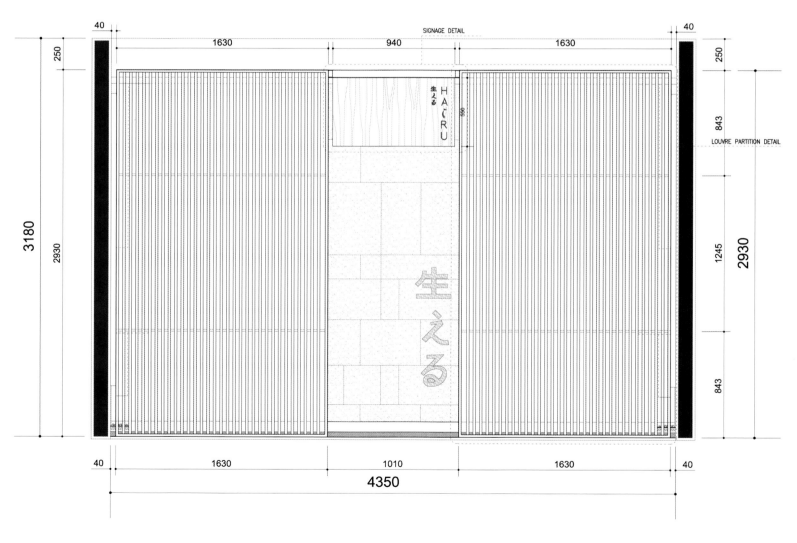

SIGNAGE DETAIL

生える H A 乙 R U

LOUVRE PARTITION DETAIL

生える

3 | SECTION A-A
1:20

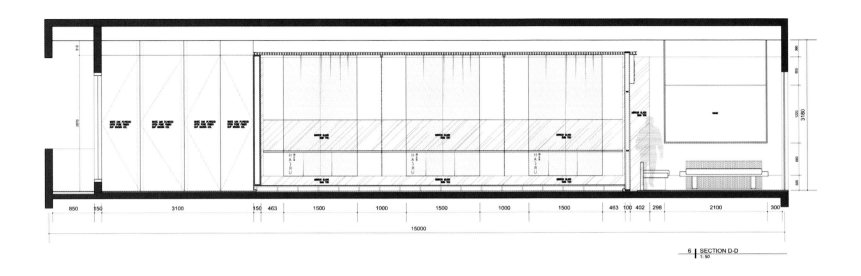

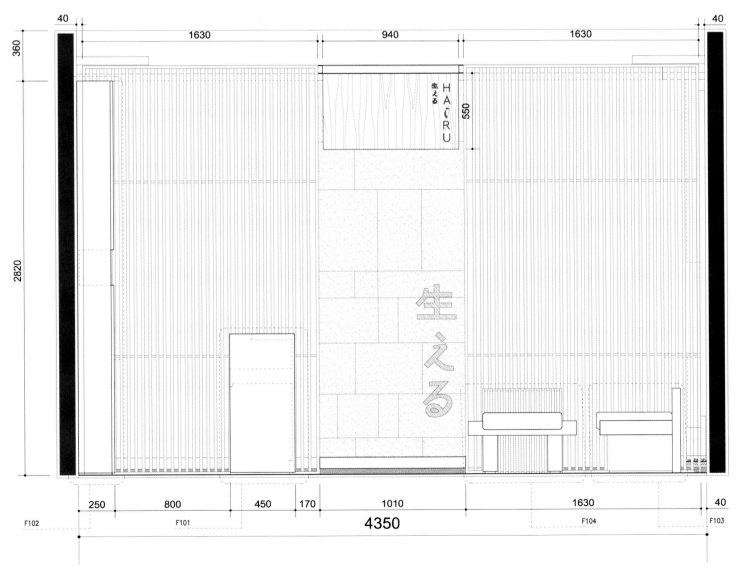

HAIRU

生える

Studio Kaze Paulista

Location: São Paulo, Brazil   Area: 335m²   Photography: Fran Parente

FGMF arquitetos

Founded in 1999, Forte, Gimenes & Marcondes Ferraz (FGMF) has shown in these few years the ability and flexibility to deal with a wide range of design types and scales.

Based on the partners' international and academic experience, the studio pursues a different and fresh approach to every design proposed. There are no pre-determined formulae or strict method defined – we start always from scratch and make the design process our research tool for a brand new vision of the city.

We are proud to have earned several relevant national architectural prizes, mostly awarded by the Brazilian Institute of Architects (IAB-SP). Such prizes stimulate our passion and focus on creative and efficient designs.

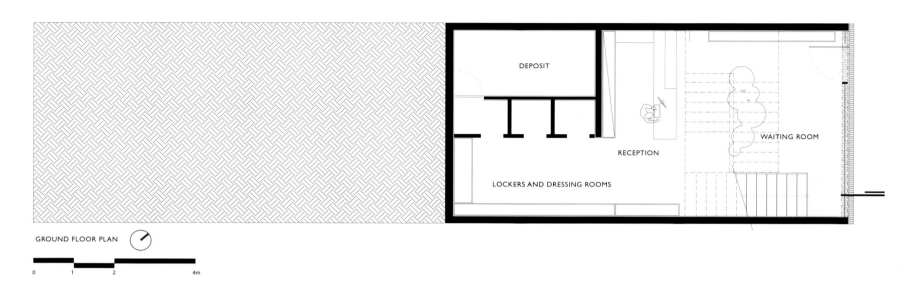

GROUND FLOOR PLAN

DEPOSIT

RECEPTION

WAITING ROOM

LOCKERS AND DRESSING ROOMS

0   1   2   4m

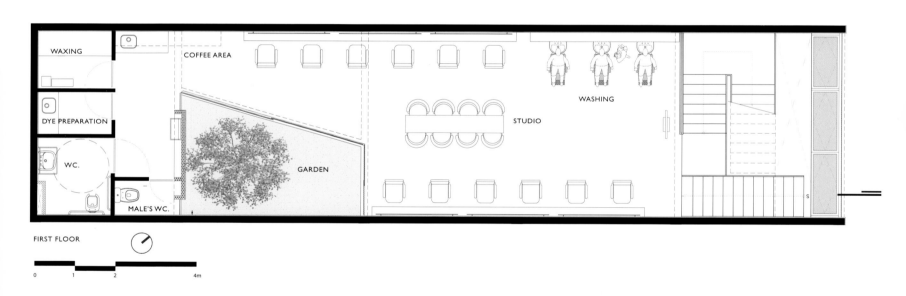

FIRST FLOOR

WAXING

COFFEE AREA

DYE PREPARATION

WC.

MALE'S WC.

GARDEN

STUDIO

WASHING

0   1   2   4m

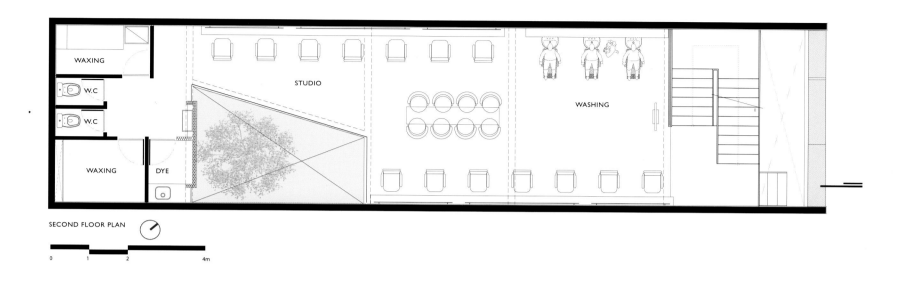

SECOND FLOOR PLAN

0   1   2   4m

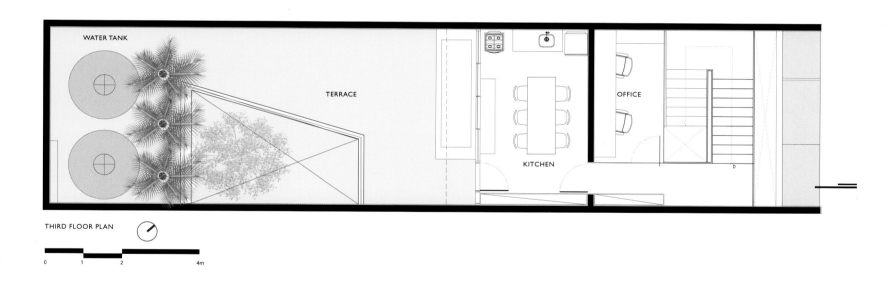

THIRD FLOOR PLAN

0   1   2   4m

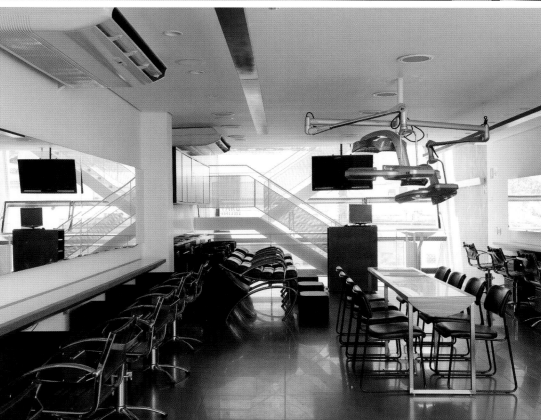

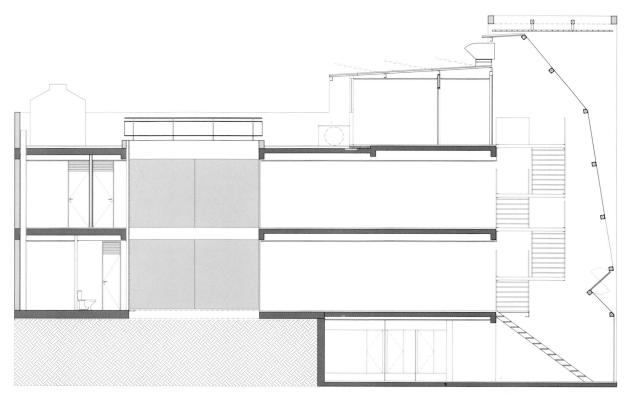

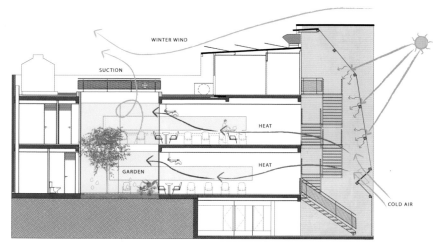

DIAGRAM - WINTER

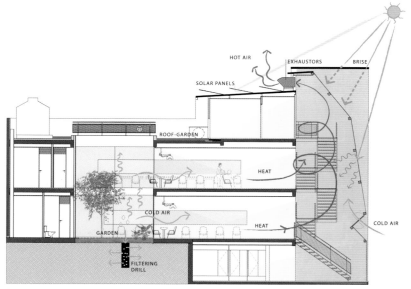

DIAGRAM - SUMMER

The program solicited by the client was a commercial space, which would be the seventh hair salon for chain located in the city of São Paulo. The building should be designed according to the aesthetic language developed by FGMF for the Kaze salon at Mooca neighborhood, in 2004, which became a symbol and standard for the entire chain.

The Kaze salon Paulista unit was therefore established on a small and narrow lot, semi-detached on both sides in which the dimensions of a previous existing building could not be changed because of a change in São Paulo construction legislation. Due to the minimal dimensions, the four floors of the building and the need for daylight, the facade composed by angled glass plates and the atrium gained great importance. The facade is the element which gives a contemporary look to the building, as its faceted form turns into a powerful lantern for the city at night. The atrium at the center of the building runs through all floors. Its main feature is a big panel made of ceramic tiles, designed by the plastic artist Fábio Flaks. It has become the area where clients lay their eyes while getting a haircut.

The spaces are organized in a simple way along four floors which communicate by a metal staircase on their frontal portion. The lower floor contains the reception and changing rooms. There are on the second and third floors different areas for haircut, washing, hair coloring, epilation, bathrooms, and pantry. On the fourth floor is the administration.

As well as a means for natural illumination, the glass facade is part of a controlled ventilation and passive temperature control system. Some window panes can be opened, allowing the passage of air through all the internal environment, cooling it on its way to exhausters on the last floor.

The small sized lot allowed the building to merge with its urban environment, semi-detached as it is, but at the same time it is able to show individuality in the contrast with the surrounding buildings, qualifying the neighborhood in which it is settled.

CARDIA AILE

Design Agency: ICHIRO NISHIWAKI DESIGN OFFICE INC.   Client: owner of beauty salon   Photography: Nacasa&Partners Inc.

ICHIRO
NISHIWAKI

Born in Tokyo, Japan.
Worked as interior designer at IIJIMA DESIGN after graduating from Kuwasawa Design School.
In 1991, founded ICHIRO NISHIWAKI DESIGN OFFICE INC.
In 1997, founded N-Planning.
Sevral prize of "JCD design Award" and "NASHOP Lighting Awards" etc.
Design policy "not only make the client pleased by producing shop,but also
make the shop doing good business", always consider about the shop after building.

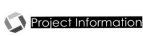
Project Information

This is a reconstructed property which was built by renovating an existing three-floor building.

The building structure and external walls are already completed, and opening sections are recreated by original designing. Sign planning is also applied to this property with great boldness. As there are few buildings which have exquisite designing in the neighborhood, it has an overwhelming advantage for the recognition and the presence of the building from a long distance. Because opening sections are narrow and have long structures in the back, the designers used the continued layout of fixed surfaces as the design components and constructed a further depth feel using their coexistence with the slim louvers which are arranged at even intervals for the feeling of private life. This has further increased the depth feel.

The designers relocated the stairway to the place near the entrance considering the easiness for customers to go upstairs. In addition, the designers designed each floor using different materials to give the shop a dual image and made the interior design according to customer's preferences. Rosewood materials are used to make it coexist with the clear glass structures with tapestry shapes and produce a modern space structure with magnitude. It should be a successful business model with no shops with similar images in the neighborhood.

D.MooD

Location: Viterbo, Italy   Project Manager: Giulio Patrizi Desgin Office   Photography: Alessandro Guadagni

Giulio Patrizi Portrai

Graduating in Industrial Design at the Accademia di Belle Arti - where to date he maintains an active lecturing collaboration - Giulio Patrizi's long, initial working experience was carried out at Massimiliano Fuksas' Studio in Rome. After his scholarship at the Politecnico di Milano, where he completed the specialization course "Hotel Experience Design", he also had an active role on a number of projects at the 3rd Architecture Biennale in Rotterdam, deeply involved in international urban planning workshops hosted by the Architecture Faculty TU Delft in Rotterdam.

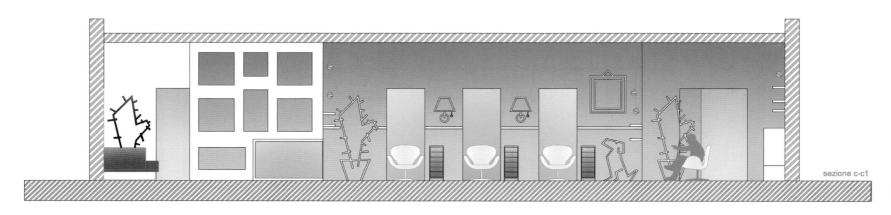

sezione c-c1

prospetto vetrine

Project Information

The Italian designer Giulio Patrizi are designing the interior project for a new hair salon in Italy, that will be opened the in August.

Designed for young talent hairdresser Daniele Luzzitelli, the D. MooD has an interior designed around the home furniture idea. Giulio Patrizi has achieved a series of wall drawings which was then declined on various icons. The fresh and cool hairdresser'style is also shown on the cool interior concept.

The D. MooD is the newest Italian Daniele Luzzitelli hair salon in Viterbo City.

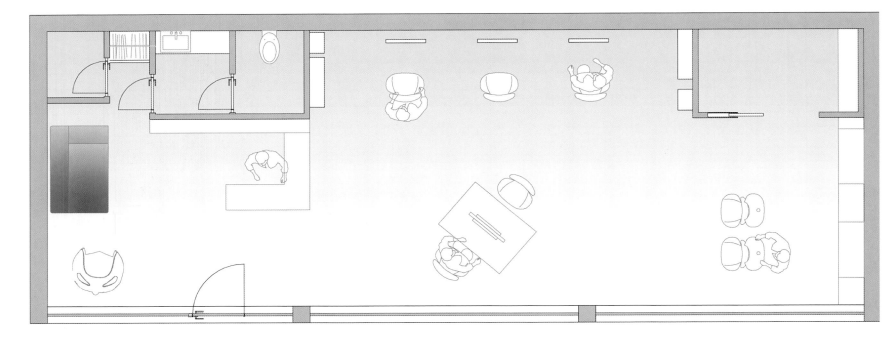

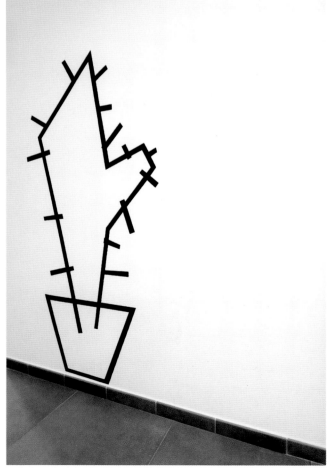

ATELIER LORIS

Location: Tuscania, Italy   Project Manager: Giulio Patrizi Desgin Office   Photography: Renzo Zecchini

Giulio Patrizi Portrai

Graduating in Industrial Design at the Accademia di Belle Arti - where to date he maintains an active lecturing collaboration - Giulio Patrizi's long, initial working experience was carried out at Massimiliano Fuksas' Studio in Rome. After his scholarship at the Politecnico di Milano, where he completed the specialization course "Hotel Experience Design", he also had an active role on a number of projects at the 3rd Architecture Biennale in Rotterdam, deeply involved in international urban planning workshops hosted by the Architecture Faculty TU Delft in Rotterdam.

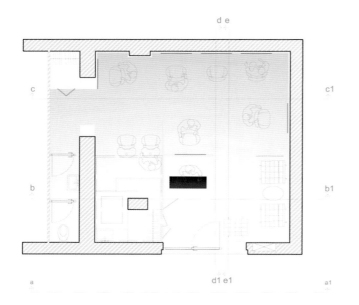

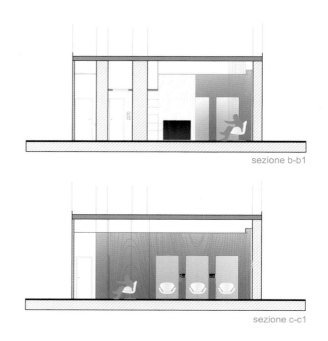

sezione b-b1

sezione c-c1

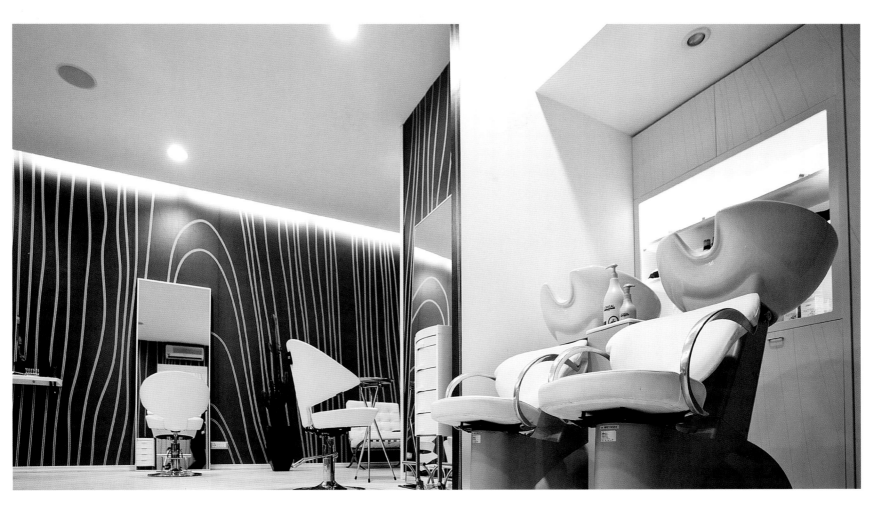

Project Information

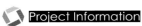

Atelier Loris is the latest space of the Italian hairdresser Simone Lippi. Hosted in the old Etruscan town of Tuscania placed in the center of Italy, this innovative space designed by the designer Giulio Patrizi it's contemporary and minimalist.

ARKHE

Location: Japan   Constructor: Kitai Corporation + Deecs   Photography: Nacasa & Partners Inc.

viewfile

Moriyuki Ochiai (Architect,Designer)
1973 Born in Tokyo,Japan
2007 Established MORIYUKI OCHIAI ARCHITECTS / TWOPLUS-A

Project Information

ARKHE is the project for a beauty salon using "water" as its main theme.

As water is also the source of life, the "recyclable aluminum" sheet decorates the ceiling by filling it in forms of luscious and elegant lines. Not only does the raw aluminum material come to life by this method, but it links the flow of water and the flow of hair. The walls are painted in a silver shade that mimics the glimmering reflection of light on the surface of water.

This space features a ceiling made of aluminium that reflects the calm – yet sometimes tempestuous – movements of flowing water. The appearance of the aluminum changes just like the lively movement of water.

In the cutting area the ceiling is high and the flow of the water is calm; in the central passage area the ceiling height varies significantly and the flow becomes tempestuously; in the waiting area the ceiling is low, and so it changes freely, taking the desirable atmosphere and required function of each space into account. In addition, the ceiling responds directly to the shades of light used, from bright white during the day to more emotional purple and blue hues by night.

Guests can experience multiple complexities of space depending on their position of observation and the time of the day.

This room conveys a simple and clear image of using water, the origin of life, for a beauty salon striving for fundamental beauty.

("Arkhe" refers to the ancient belief that water is the source of all creation.)

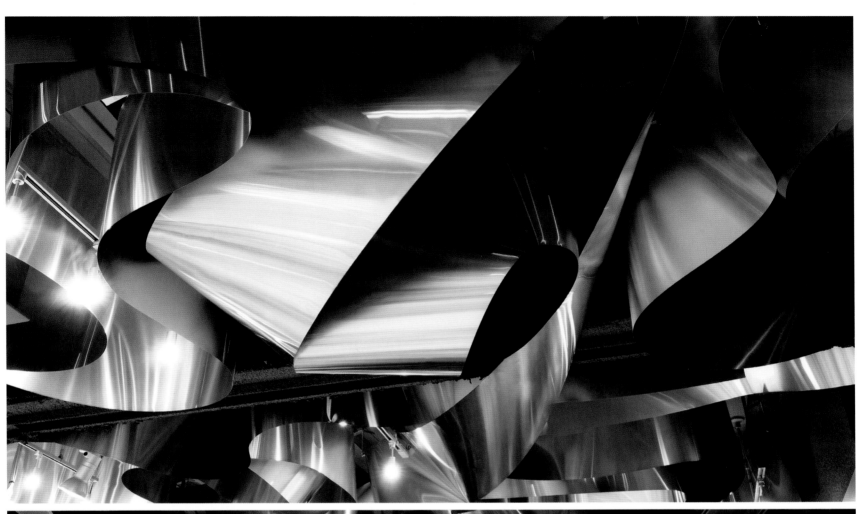

Cure Salon Monsieur

Designer: Shuzo Okabe   Photography: Yusuke Wakabayashi

upsetters architects

"Observe the city and reconstruct the city scape" is the slogan of upsetters architects. They declare it as their concept and they are inter-disciplinarily working on architectural design, interior design, event management etc., which all relate to urban activities. During the past few years, they have been selected for JCD Design Award Gold Prize, Good Design Award, Kids Design Award and so on.

Shuzo Okabe is director/architect of upsetters architects, Satoshi Uekawa is project manager and Tokuhiro Barada is a member of the Board. Of course, there are also other members, such as Tomoaki Ishiguro and Hideyuki Yamazawa.

Their field is very widely, including Architectural Design, Urban Design, Interior Design, Product Design and so on. Through the continuous efforts, upsetters architects becomes more and more famous.

 Project Information

A complex of a beauty salon and a cafe, whose site has a narrow frontage.

The site is a little way off the main shopping street and on a lane. In addition, it is narrow and deep, which the Japanese call "unagino-nedoko" (means "a bed for an eel"). The client desired it to be like a retreat. So the design focused on utilising the depth of the site sandwiched between two buildings and creating an interior space in which people can feel light. Thus the design divided the building into three parts and slightly shifted each other. Additionally, the design used different materials for each part and alternate their roof pitches so that people can feel it extending far back. Furthermore, the design put its entrance on the side and people just feel what is happening inside in its front. This should make people want to peep into the room.

The space for hair dressing is located in the middle and has the other two parts' exterior walls as its interior wall. Moreover, it is facing the small garden and the customers will see it over the mirrors. Consequently, they can enjoy being hair dressed inside the building just like outdoors.

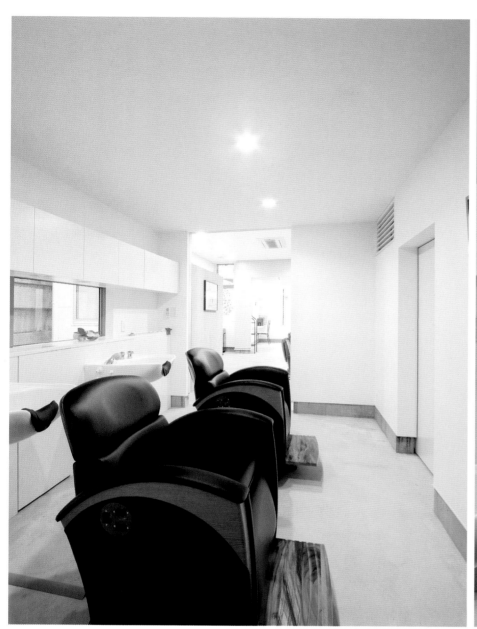

GARDEN by be area

Designer: Kazutoyo Yamamoto   Client: BE AREA   Photography: Toshiyuki Yano / Nacasa&Partners Inc.

Dessence co,ltd.

1976 Born in Saitama, Japan.1999-2003 Founded CDL.
During this time I traveled the world,exposing me to the design and architecture of other cultures,which influenced me as well.
2005 Founded Dessence co,ltd. Focus on designing and constructing residential,commercial,office and products design.

On the other side of the facade's large picture window stands the expansiveness of a wedding hall. It can be said that the focal point of the salon is the large tree that almost jumps out at the viewer. When one enters through the main entrance, a pewter counter stands in silence. Even though the pewter is a metal it creates an expression of a dewy like moistness. Across from this counter sits a low table. This table is integrated in with a large planter that secures the large warm green tree. Thus giving the waiting customers a relaxed atmosphere to sit back in and almost believe that they are bathing in some rich green forest, causing them to lose all track of waiting time. As far as the cutting area goes, the design wonted to create a relative sense of privacy. That is, relative to the sitting customer. Here the design made partitions out of plants and set them at intervals so that the sitting customer would feel perfectly secure. These plants are set to look as if they were descending from the heavens.

As one further proceeds into the back of the salon it is almost as if you are entering into the depths of a narrowing cave. Though, not necessarily claustrophobic, because when you pass through a doorway you receive an totally opposite response. Here you feel as if the skies have opened.

Architecturally speaking it is an enclosed space but with the windowed ceiling you are connected to the outside. My presentation is perfected here by covering the ceiling with a thick growing green through which a flood of sunlight is emitted. My overall idea of this project was to take plants that are normally seen on the outside and transplant them to the inside and provide that strong sense of relaxation that only a green forest has to offer.

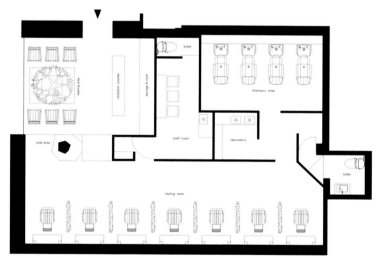

S=1/50

Hue Ponsonby

Design Agency: PA to Mark Gascoigne   Client: Hue   Photography: Emily Andrews

Mark Gascoigne
Naomi Rushmer

Gascoigne Associates is a multi-disciplinary design and consultancy office that integrates architecture with interior design, lighting design, and retail branding consultancy services.

Gascoigne specialize in creating new retail brands and re-imaging of existing ones in order to best present them to their other markets and thereby maximize revenues. Design services are provided for a wide range of projects, both nationally and internationally. Clients include many of the most successful retailers from Australasia as well as several multinational corporates such as Toyota and Westfield. Current project budgets range from $200 thousand to $95 million. Gascoigne is currently designing projects throughout Australia and New Zealand as well as selected projects in Asia.

2010 marked Gascoigne Associates' 25th year in business. We will shortly be up to our 2000th project.

We have received over 120 design awards. This year also marks the 20th year of our involvement with some of our clients. To date by working closely with these and other clients, they have all achieved increased turnover and profit. We believe that it is this close working relationship that makes all the difference.

Project Information

Hue Ponsonby is the second of a start-up chain of color-only hair salons that targets women who have their hair colored regularly but wish to avoid high salon prices. A number of Hues will be set up quickly and cost-effectively in existing buildings. To facilitate this, the fixtures that make up the fit-out are simple white items, designed to sit within existing spaces rather than being custom-built to fit.

The way that a salon works had to be reinvented to maximize efficiency while considering the needs of the client. Typically a salon's customer is moved a number of times during their treatment and sits facing a wall for much of it. At Hue the customer sits either at the "Color Table" or in the "Color Lounge" where they can interact with other clients, while the colorist comes to them. The experience is therefore more like a café rather than a typical hair salon. The sliding mirrors give clients the choice of either watching their treatment or chatting with other customers.

The building was an old workshop structure whose interior of exposed brick and timber forms a nice backdrop to the simple, white fixtures within. The existing plasterboard walls have been covered in vinyl graphics that reinforce the Hue brand and bring color to the space. The brand colors, chosen for the warmth and vibrancy they impart, were repeated in the suspended, acrylic screen defining the Customer Lounge. This semi-enclosed space allows clients to feel connected to the salon activity while separate enough to relax. Each Hue has a distinctly different feel by virtue of emphasizing the features of the diverse spaces they inhabit while retaining the distinctive branding, which remains immediately recognisable.

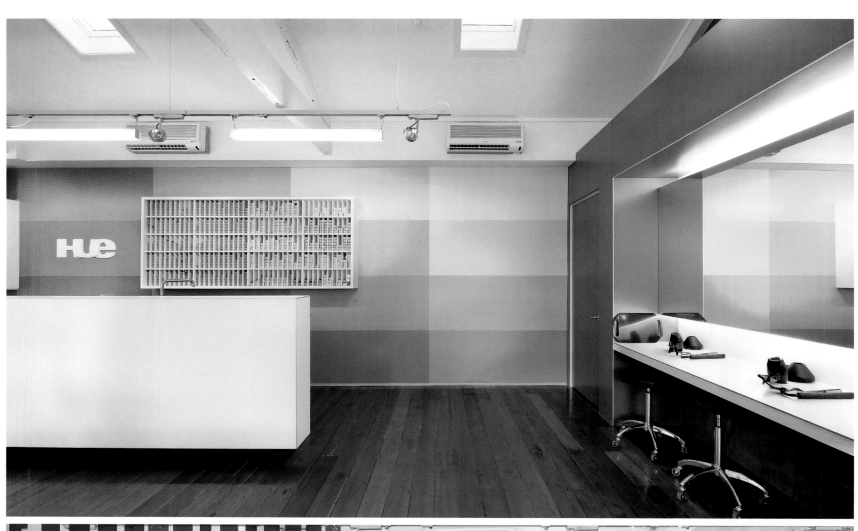

Style Club

Location: Dublin, Ireland   Design Agency : Garry Cohn for Douglas Wallace   Client: Peter Mark   Photography: Conor Horgan

Garry Cohn

More than 20 years experience in the interior design industry creating interiors that are sophisticated, cutting edge and setting new trends throughout the industry. His use of shapes and proportions truly stimulates the imagination. It has been described as the "haute couture of the interior design world" with an intelligent use of style, form and function. Garry Cohn has won many awards, the most recent being nominated as one of the top interior designers by Andrew Martin 2010 Interior Design Review. Garry Cohn's background is well verse with an extensive knowledge in designing for residential, retail, commercial, hospitality, leisure and aviation. Successfully ran his own design company in New York City and a professor at the Fashion Institute of Technology. Designing is a passion in the Garry Cohn's international design company and this is present in the attention to detail given to every project.

LINE OF PREVIOUSLY PROPOSED THIRD FLOOR SUBMITTED UNDER PLANNING REFERENCE 5111/06.

* NOTE NO REVISIONS PROPOSED TO FRONT ELEVATION PROPOSED THIRD FLOOR WILL NOT BE VISIBLE.

FINISH THIRD FLOOR SLAB LEVEL = 23.58m

FINISH SECOND FLOOR SLAB LEVEL = 19.32m

FINISH FIRST FLOOR SLAB LEVEL = 15.05m

FINISH GROUND FLOOR SLAB LEVEL = 10.78m

FINISH BASEMENT SLAB LEVEL = 7.77m

STYLE CLUB
CREATIVE CENTER
COLLEGE OF HAIRDRESSING

LOCATION OF SITE NOTICE.

Ground Level:10.13

A new style is born that takes Punk, Japanimation, New Wave, Memphis, Classical Design and a lot of imagination mixed with a 21st century twist. It is refreshing to see Ireland in the lime light creating a new innovative design style.

The design is not minimal. Less is not more in this space—more is more and fun at the same time. Entering the traditional building you know that there is something special going on before you set foot into the space. From the street you see a wild linticular (3-dimensional graphics) ceiling in a crazy pattern with vibrant salmon colored walls and bright white traditional moldings.

Entering the salon feels like falling into Alice in Wonderland, where this time she is a "punk rocker". It's real eye candy. Patterns clash and work at the same time. Colors collide that should never go together, and yet somehow work. Shapes and forms that don't belong with each other are living happily side but side, it's ingenious. Everywhere you turn is a new experience. It's as if you are in a new space at every angle you turn.

The design is clever with its wall of convex mirrors against a stripe patterned wall that sits next to, yes, a tartan wall—next to blue stylized clouds! This is all offset by a pink giraffe-skin printed ceiling complete with pink giraffe-skin marshmallow shapes. You just have to see it to believe it. Whether you want to admit it or not, it is an amazing design with the highest standards of detail and finishes. There is real sophistication in the project: thing clash and work all at the same time. There an understanding of proportion and balance of color. This is not something that can be easily achieved and the Style Club succeeds with flying colors.

Whether you like the design or not, once you walk into the Style Club you cannot help but put a smile on your face.

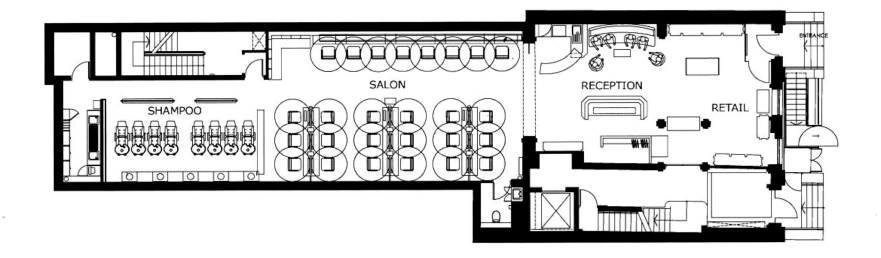

STYLE CLUB

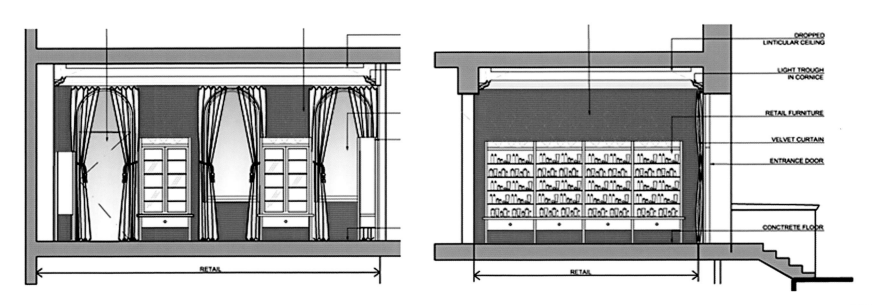

RETAIL

DROPPED
LINTICULAR CEILING

LIGHT TROUGH
IN CORNICE

RETAIL FURNITURE

VELVET CURTAIN

ENTRANCE DOOR

CONCTRETE FLOOR

RETAIL

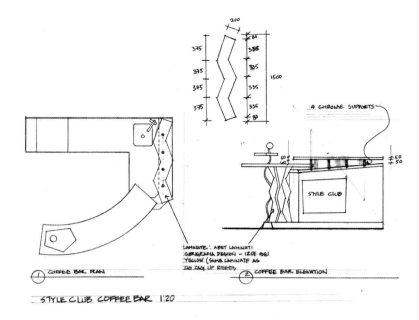

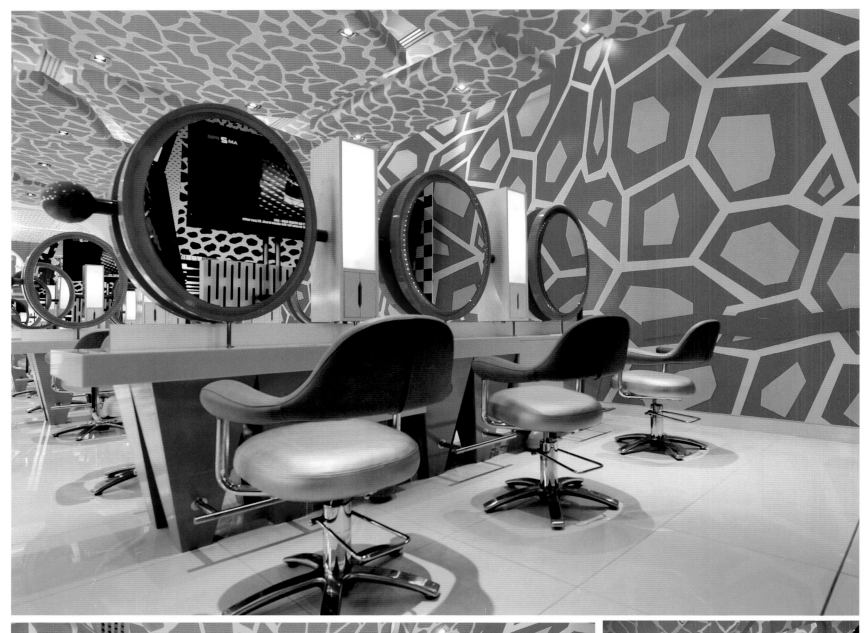

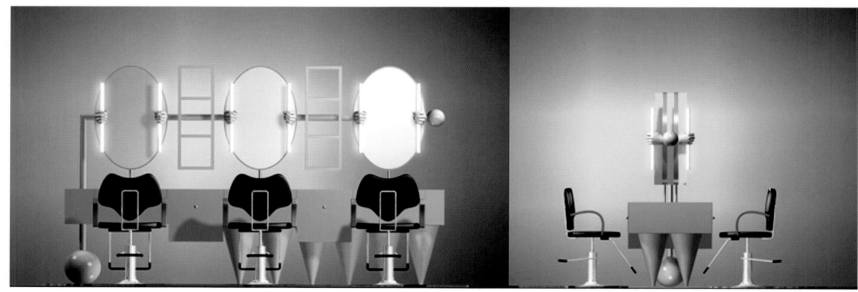

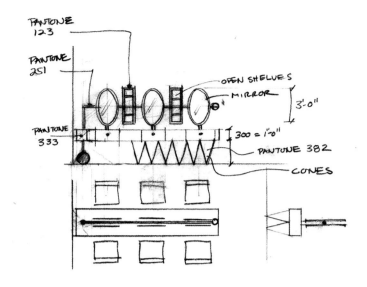

Noriaki Takeda
Ikuma Yoshizawa

Hair&Heal CaCa

Design Agency: PROCESS5 DESIGN   Client: Hair&Heal CaCa   Photography: PROCESS5 DESIGN

PROCESS5 DESIGN was started as PROCESS5 by Noriaki Takeda and Ikuma Yoshizawa in 1999.
The office was established as PROCESS5 DESIGN in 2009 in Osaka, Japan.

PROCESS5 DESIGN designs architecture, interior, and graphic which valued the concept regardless of use.

Noriaki Takeda was born in Osaka in 1980. He received his degree from the architectural course of Kinki University in 2003. After worked for MARIO DELblank MARE(2003-2006), he established office.

Ikuma Yoshizawa was born in Nara in 1980. He received his degree from the architectural course of Kinki University in 2003. After worked for AMORPHE Takeyama & Associates(2003-2009), he established office.

Project Information

A quiet residential area amid a rich natural environment in Toyokawa City, Aichi Prefecture. This plan is of a hair salon facing a prefectural highway which is the main community road for nearby residents. The young owner is in his 20's and preparing to open a hair salon in Toyokawa, the town of his residence, with the goal of materializing his beauty ideals.

The owner's request was to create a hair salon that is natural and calm, a place where nearby residents can casually gather. In addition, location, main target customers, existing tenant situation, indoor heating environment, cost and other issues needed to be addressed. In order to come up with simplest answer to the above, and to make the salon a place where customers can feel comfortable, the designs sought to establish a certain rule as a solution.

In particular, a rule was created for the cross section and planar surface for wooden boards with uniform width and thickness. In the cross section plan, the wooden boards would be angled differently so that there would be an open view towards the top and bottom. As a result, the customers seated in the salon chairs do not have to make eye contact with the other customers, and despite the limited space, the salon can have an open atmosphere through the openings and connections towards the top and bottom. Additionally, by converting the existing air conditioning in order to keep costs down, and by circulating the air through the opening of the wooden boards at the top and bottom, the salon environment would be a comfortable one.

In the floor plan, the wooden walls partitioning off each booth would be angled differently to one another so as to have a narrow entrance in relation to the floor of the existing building which widens as you move further in. As a result, you can walk in from a narrow entrance to a wide space, where each space is connected at the same time having a private room atmosphere. The private room atmosphere is created with consideration to the owner's desire that each customer can relax without being conscious of others. At the same time, according to this plan, the semi-private atmosphere enables the assistant to follow-up on the hair dresser without delay, which would be difficult in a completely-private space.

Through the simple solution of creating a cross section and planar rule for the wooden boards, a hair salon was created which was named "Hair & Heal Caca" by the owner. By adding "Hair & Heal" to the salon name, the implication is that the completed space is not just a hair designing spot where nearby residents gather, but also a location where you can forget your day to day busy lifestyle and be healed.

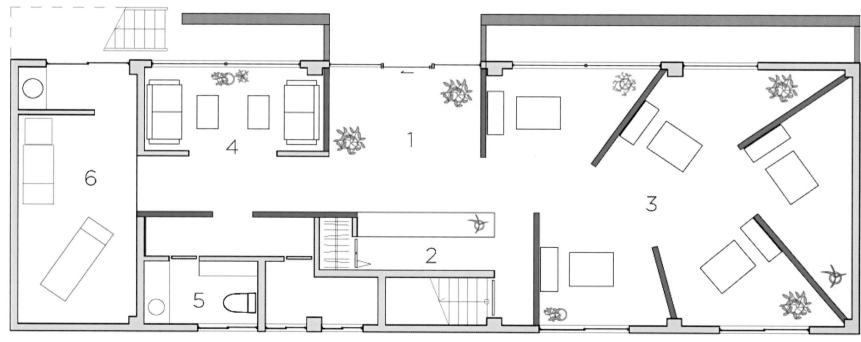

1:200 Plan

1.Entrance   2.Reception   3.Cut space   4.Waiting space   5.WC   6.Shampoo space

PRIVATE DESIGN

Design Agency: PROCESS5 DESIGN   Client: PRIVATE DESIGN   Photography: PROCESS5 DESIGN

Noriaki Takeda
Ikuma Yoshizawa

PROCESS5 DESIGN was started as PROCESS5 by Noriaki Takeda and Ikuma Yoshizawa in 1999.
The office was established as PROCESS5 DESIGN in 2009 in Osaka, Japan.

PROCESS5 DESIGN designs architecture, interior, and graphic which valued the concept regardless of use.

Noriaki Takeda was born in Osaka in 1980. He received his degree from the architectural course of Kinki University in 2003. After worked for MARIO DELblank MARE(2003-2006), he established office.

Ikuma Yoshizawa was born in Nara in 1980. He received his degree from the architectural course of Kinki University in 2003. After worked for AMORPHE Takeyama & Associates(2003-2009), he established office.

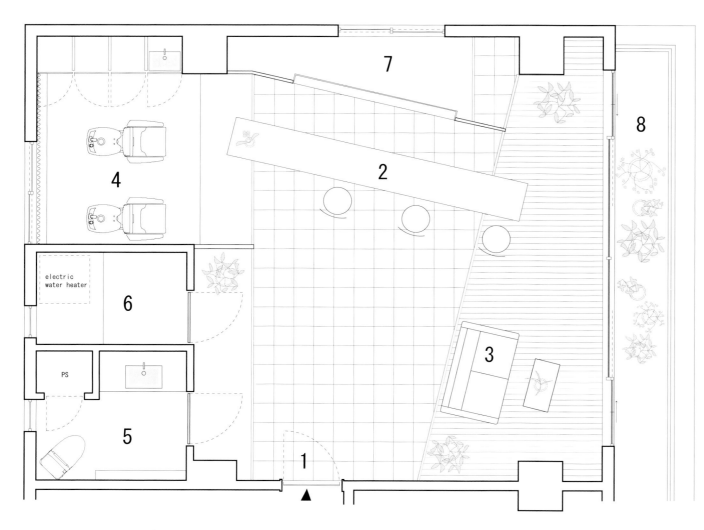

1:Entrance

2:Styling space

3:Waiting space

4:Shampoo space

5:Lavatory

6:Storage

7:Staff room

8:Terrace

PLAN (1/100)

Minatomachi, Yokohama. "Private Design" opened in a quite location somewhat away from the row of restaurants. This is the first store opened by the owner, and his desire is to work in a comfortable atmosphere interacting with the customers. This derives from the owner's beauty concept in which the act of hair trimming would contribute to the designing of a part of the customers' life. In order to make the somewhat nerve-wrecking act of going to a hair salon into more of a casual act, the designers suggested a "bar-like hair salon." From this concept, a conversational-type hair salon, similar to having a conversation with the bartender at a "favorite hangout bar," would result.

The store is occupied by a large 4.5 meters trimming counter resembling a bar counter. By inserting an original mirror into the groove of the counter, the bar atmosphere is transformed into a hair salon atmosphere.
Additionally, in order to balance the lighting to reflect both the bar atmosphere and the hair salon atmosphere, custom-made lighting was created.

Natural color tones of white and brown are integrated into the space, with the owner's favorite color red and a cool light blue inserted into it.

The proposal of a "hair salon with a bar-like atmosphere," which was created as a result of fusing elements transcending the genre of a hair salon and a bar, is the answer to the owner's request to "be able to interact with each customer in comfort," achieving a space where the customer and the owner can communicate in relaxed comfort.

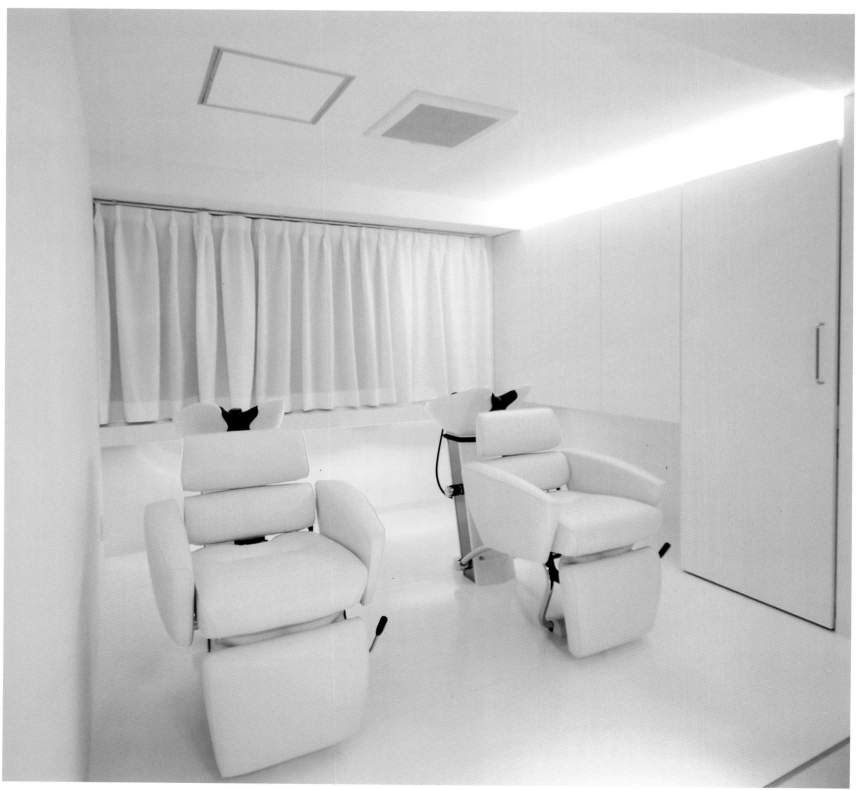

TOAST

Design Agency: ICHIRO NISHIWAKI DESIGN OFFICE INC.   Client: TOAST   Photography: Nacasa&Partners Inc.

ICHIRO
NISHIWAKI

Born in Tokyo, Japan.
Worked as interior designer at IIJIMA DESIGN after graduating from Kuwasawa Design School.
In 1991, founded ICHIRO NISHIWAKI DESIGN OFFICE INC.
In 1997, founded N-Planning.
Sevral prize of "JCD design Award" and "NASHOP Lighting Awards" etc.
Design policy "not only make the client pleased by producing shop,but also
make the shop doing good business", always consider about the shop after building.

 **Project Information**

Because one floor is leased to a single tenant, the exclusive
entrance space in front of the elevator door is rather small; which
is peculiar to this facility. However, when you walk through the
small storefront, you will find an open floor surrounded by the
glass walls and a long reception counter facing you. This counter
can be used as the bar counter for welcome drinks. The booths
in imitation of easels are aligned to face the glass wall, through
which you can overlook Aoyama. The wagons including fixture
are made of rosewood in a unified form to provide high quality
feeling of completeness. For the shampoo booths, the materials
such as stone are selected to provide an atmosphere of the
resort in the southland, accentuated by special lighting. Another
feature of this store consists in the space for after treatments;
there are several sets of sofas facing the glass wall and drinks are
served there. The chandeliers add to fashionableness and luxury
feeling to the space. Thus, this is a hair saloon of a new style.

K-two

Location: Osaka, Japan   Design Agency: designroom702 Co., Ltd.   client: K two effect co.,ltd   photography: Nacasa&Partners Inc

HIROYUKI
MATSUNAKA

Interior designer Hiroyuki Matsunaka had established a cafe called "cafe co" with its own architectural design office, with his three other friends in 1996. This new form of cafe had received a lot of attention from its creators based in Minamihorie Osaka. When the design office got off off the ground, Matsunaka wanted to get involved in the wide spectrum of designs, and launched his own architectural and interior design office called "design room 702" in 2004.

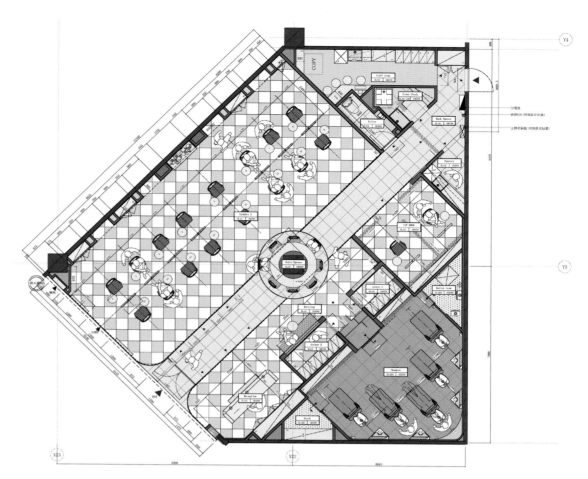

The sun and the moon, reality and imagination, they are the best relationns. This relation take in the space of the K-two Abeno branch.

The technique and the detail seen in the style of architecture of Europe made a modern space. Consecutive arcuate passage arranged at center. The cutting space composed of a consecutive arch gives space the extension in the effect of mirror. The ARTBOOK, candle holder and other objets of an overseas selection are selected in France.

All Furniture that sticks to the detail are special orders. The shampoo space is a fantastic space where the art crossing comes to the wall in a pitch-dark space.

L'Unique Hair Salon

Design Agency: **Creneau International**   Client: **L'Unique**   Photography: Philippe Van Gelooven

Creneau International

Creneau International is a Belgian concept and design consultancy and has more than 20 years of experience in realizing highly reputable projects worldwide. With offices in Hasselt and Dubai, representation in Sydney, Prague and Kiev and a production plant in Jakarta, CI is exploring its boundaries every day.

That's the corporate side, but what does it mean? Their house logo featuring two winged monkeys and the baseline "Hacitur ad astra", gives a pretty good idea: CI makes you reach for the stars. Through their design concepts, including interior design and brand image to graphic creations, their "ideas of the anti-ordinary" are stamped on the imagination of global visual communication below the line.

Modeling the intangible and transforming the tangible, that's their working domain. As atmosphere architects they thrust their way into your environment and transform your brand values and company's mission statement, into a total design concept.

Project Information

A beautiful combination of contemporary and classic elements: walls covered in retro wallpaper, clients wait for their turn in a classic couch & the dressers table sets people opposed to each other, allowing more social contact.

The table rests on one heavy twisted leg that also serves as a flower pot. The lighting is also a combination of contemporary "downlighters" with classic styled armatures. The eye catcher is the artwork on the walls: a drawing in nails and cotton, referring to hair because of its look and feel.

Palladium Pretoria

Design Agency: EFTIS

Emilio Eftychis

Since 2006, Emilio Eftychis has developed EFTIS: an interdisciplinary practice specializing in architecture, interior design, furniture creation and art direction.

He explores the relationship between rational and intuitive design processes and believes strongly in the transformative power of design. Emilio's perception of the world was enriched by travels across the globe and multicultural experiences.

Project Information

Strips of wood emanate idea of flowing hair. As seen on counters raised deck becomes a stage for the user. Wrap ceiling/wall/floor (raised) embraces user. Black polished floor tiles create illusion of weightlessness by reflections. Paisley wall paper provides an association to glamour. Shop flows onto outside astroturf patio seamlessy through glass sliding doors.

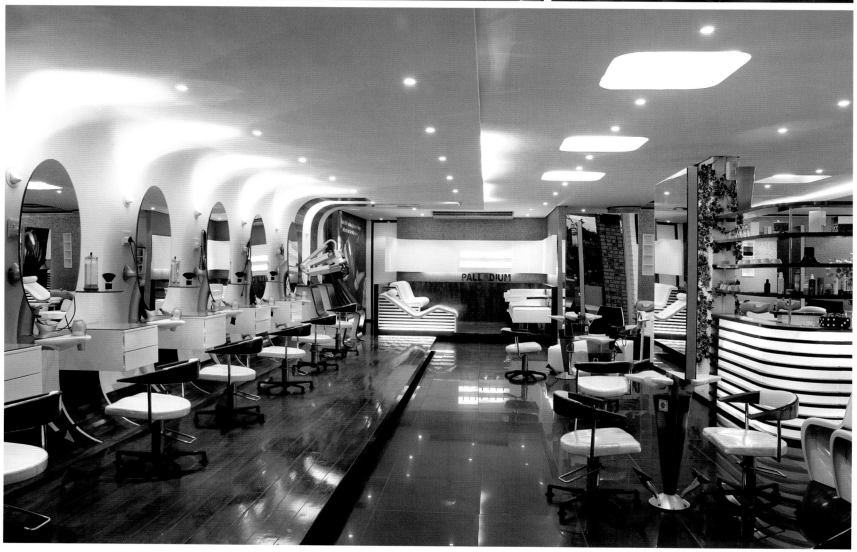

Palladium Cape Town

Design Agency: EFTIS

Emilio Eftychis

Since 2006, Emilio Eftychis has developed EFTIS: an interdisciplinary practice specializing in architecture, interior design, furniture creation and art direction.

He explores the relationship between rational and intuitive design processes and believes strongly in the transformative power of design. Emilio's perception of the world was enriched by travels across the globe and multi-cultural experiences.

 Project Information

The aim with this interior was to evolve the original design. A more subtle approach was adopted to make the necessary contextual shift. The glass sliding doors and minimal wall space posed a challenge for the placement of mirror units. However, by allowing the Cape Town skies to form a backdrop, the natural light of the environment was exploited. Wing-like bulkheads lend a sense of flight while the presence of heavy wood contrasts with the white walls and décor to create an environment that is modern, yet unyielding.

SQ1 Rouge Make-Up Lounge

Design Agency: Square One Interior Design

Square One   Square One Interior Design is a full service design firm committed to providing clients with responsive & creative design solutions backed by dedicated service and professional integrity. Passionate about design, from conception to completion, we get to the right solution through teamwork and seamless implementation.

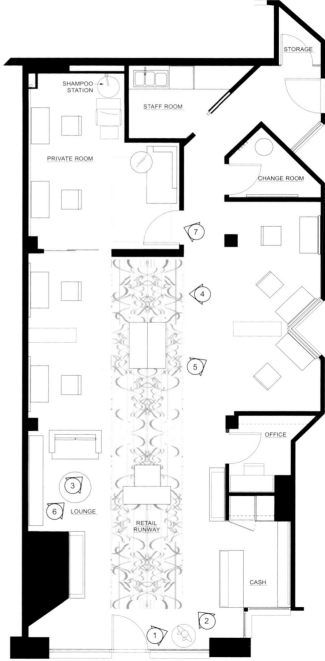

Rouge Make-Up Lounge is a prototype concept located in Yaletown, Vancouver's upscale renovated warehouse district, described as the neighborhood of choice for urban trend-setters.

This elegant, stylish space is highly focused on customers, offering exclusive services and products. A mirrored sculptural mannequin welcomes customers, and sets the mood for a glamorous, pampering experience. The hand-painted floor pattern defines the product run-way, which is reflected back, visually expanding the size of the space. Extensive use of reflective materials and surfaces emphasize that the customer is the focus. The private room offers a chic lounge space for a more exclusive experience.

Underlying the glamour is a very organized space that respects the heritage architecture of the existing warehouse building. Existing structural douglas fir beams and column are complimented by clean simple planes of the interior, and a sophisticated subtle palette.

Seashell+ Hair Salon

Design Agency: Design Quarter Studio   Art Director: Alexander Ryandi & Sharleen Sulaiman

Alexander Ryandi
Sharleen Sulaiman

Alex and Sharleen, they both graduated as Bachelor of Design majoring in Interior Design. They design spaces in every scope from residential to commercial. Creating and transforming space into useful and extra-ordinary area is their passion. At the same time, they are seeking experiences that allowing them to fully utilize their knowledge and skills as an interior designer and to work independently as a professional. Currently they are working as professional within projects in Indonesia and Singapore.

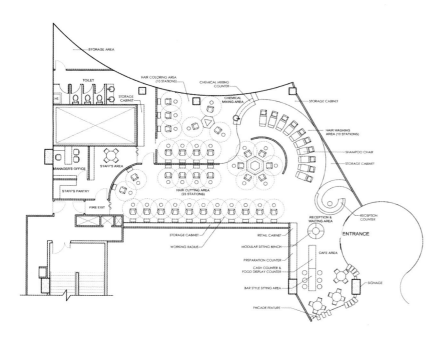

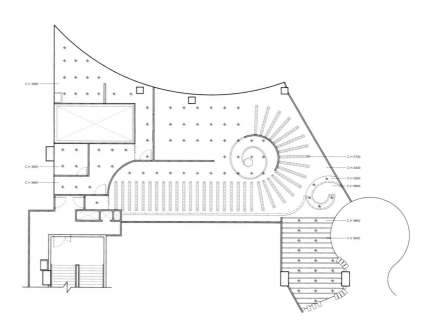

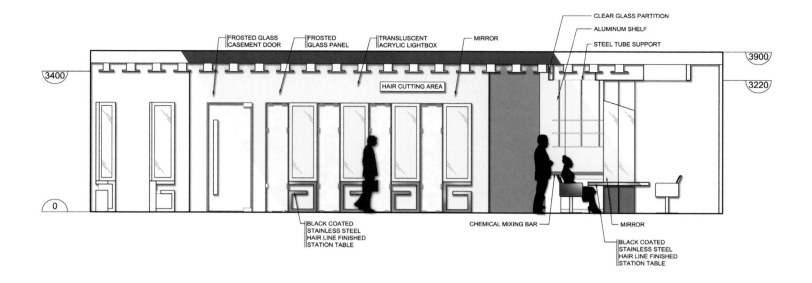

FROSTED GLASS CASEMENT DOOR
FROSTED GLASS PANEL
TRANSLUSCENT ACRYLIC LIGHTBOX
MIRROR
CLEAR GLASS PARTITION
ALUMINUM SHELF
STEEL TUBE SUPPORT

HAIR CUTTING AREA

3400
3900
3220
0

BLACK COATED STAINLESS STEEL HAIR LINE FINISHED STATION TABLE
CHEMICAL MIXING BAR
MIRROR
BLACK COATED STAINLESS STEEL HAIR LINE FINISHED STATION TABLE

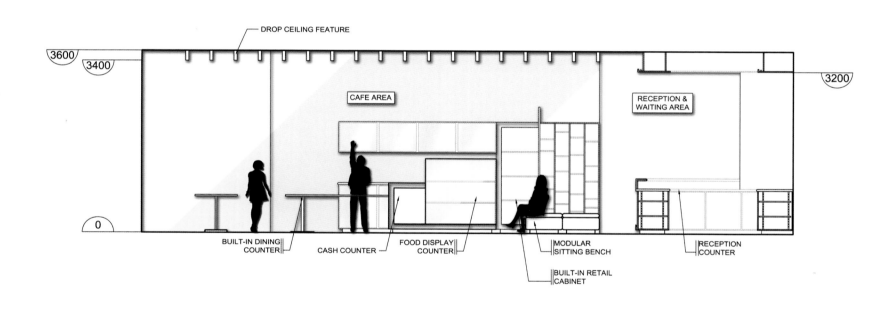

DROP CEILING FEATURE

3600
3400
3200
0

CAFE AREA
RECEPTION & WAITING AREA

BUILT-IN DINING COUNTER
CASH COUNTER
FOOD DISPLAY COUNTER
MODULAR SITTING BENCH
RECEPTION COUNTER
BUILT-IN RETAIL CABINET

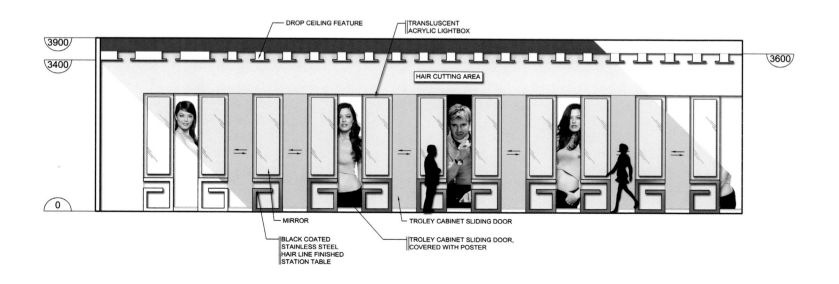

DROP CEILING FEATURE
TRANSLUSCENT ACRYLIC LIGHTBOX

3900
3400
3600
0

HAIR CUTTING AREA

MIRROR
TROLEY CABINET SLIDING DOOR
BLACK COATED STAINLESS STEEL HAIR LINE FINISHED STATION TABLE
TROLEY CABINET SLIDING DOOR, COVERED WITH POSTER

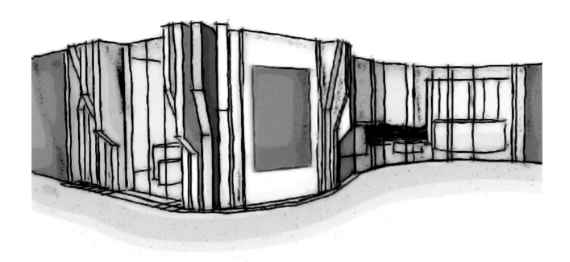

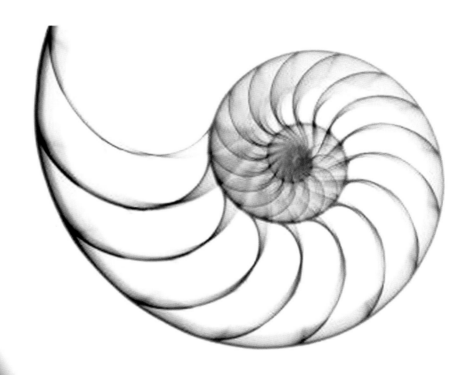

The inspiration came from the fact that seashell has so many layers. The outer layer is said as a hard and protective layer because it has a function to protect the body of a sea creature that lives inside it. The inner layer of seashell which is a soft, white, and thin layer, inspired us to use white as the main color scheme for the salon to represent the purity and simplicity.

Therefore the designers proposed to use some of the seashell elements in the design, such as the principle of layers and curves. Besides playing with that element, the designers are also played with angular shapes supported with various ceiling height and some features to create the sense of futuristic yet dynamic feeling inside the space. As per the concept of sea shell, they are trying to combine everything in soft edges as they found out that sea shell has edgeless. The color schemes the designers proposed was white and the shades to give cool, luxury, and bright atmosphere inside the salon.

KIZUKI + LIM12

TERUHIRO YANAGI-
HARA

Teruhiro Yanagihara was born in 1976 in Kagawa, Japan. After graduating from Osaka University of Art in 1999, he started to work independently and established his own company in Osaka in 2002. Since then, he has been working in the fields of interior and product design and art/creative direction for national and international clients, such as LESS IS MORE (LIM) Group (Japan), KARIMOKU (Japan), KIMURA GLASS (Japan), MATER (Denmark), OFFECCT (Sweden), PALLUCCO (Italy). His works have been the subject of numerous exhibitions in Japan and Europe and has been published in various books and major magazines. He was nominated Elle Decor Young Talent of the Year 2010. Staff members: David Glaettli, design direction; Maiko Okada, design management.

Project Information

The latest branch of the rapidly growing Japanese company "Less is More" is located in the prestigious Raffles Hotel in the centre of Singapore. The very contemporary setting, merged into the large history-charged space, reflects the spirit of the young Japanese stylists, who came to tropically hot Singapore with their "cool" styles and ideas. A "glacier"-like structure dominates the space and separates it into reception, cutting and shampooing area. In the cutting area large pivotable wings with mirrors fold out of the wall. When they are closed they flush into the wall, allowing the room to become a spacious location for events and concerts. The timbered reception "hut", includes a small gallery space that works as a platform for local artists.

Ruben Woods

Peter Masters

Award winning furniture designer Peter Masters combines beauty and resourcefulness within the mass-produced market, alongside the exquisite craftsmanship and resilience of bespoke products available for commission.

Peter approaches the industry with the aim of incorporating a variety of materials and techniques and wherever possible using sustainable materials. The beauty of Master's designs is the ability to achieve structurally striking and complex forms using the most simple of techniques and processes. He prides himself on re-evaluating existing manufacturing techniques and material capabilities, like creating the afore-mentioned table using a machine used to manufacture violins, allowing him to form unusual objects without using complex manufacturing techniques.

Peter places high importance on all of his pieces be-

ing handmade here in the UK, believing we have all the resources to manufacture here, and as a result reducing manufacturing costs.

However, all of this does put boundaries on the creative and manufacturing process, from which Peter thrives, "I feel boundaries channel the design

Project Information

Reuben Wood Hair Salon in the Northern Quarter of Manchester city centre has recently undergone a transformation at the hands of the Master(s), providing a worthy showcase for the talents that Masters has combined to establish a functional mix of elegance, funk and hi-tech.

Masters has used his trademark curves on the mirrors, which cleverly conceal the necessary day-to-day products and gadgets used to create the cutting edge designs produced by Reuben Wood and his top-notch team of stylists and color technicians. The mirrors are removable so the salon interior can be changed whilst keep the ambience. Splashes of bright colors, green, pink and blue, balance the larger areas of black and white, making interesting focal points through the reflective walls.

To counteract the reflective surfaces, the rest of the furnishings and décor were kept simple and minimalist to make the most of the available space and to keep the salon looking light, airy and efficient.

Masters' Horse design was the inspiration for the long blue work surface, which dissects the length of the salon, successfully combining form and function. Masters utilizes a range of materials, methods and technologies in his designs. He is equally at home when laminating plywood, casting resins and metals, fabricating plastics and upholstery as he is proficient in using a machine specifically created for making violins or when hand-crafting custom designs from green materials.

Bonce

Location: UK   Designer : Aston & Fincher

GAMMA &amp   GAMMA &amp officially born 30 years ago. The design team makes an expert fusion of design and production techniques, together with the historical knowledge of the profession with its own specific needs. Quality of construction as well as salon image are the key elements upon which GAMMA &amp and BROSS SPA focuses its entrepreneurial commitment. Now the company sells its upscale furniture in more than 50 countries and the distribution network has been developed in more than 30 countries.

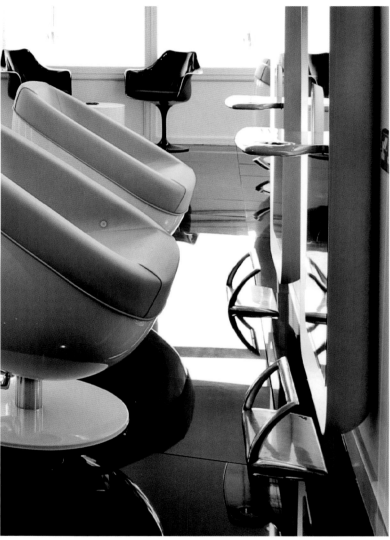

Project Information

There is absolutely nothing minimalist or boring about Bonce Hair Salon Walsall. It's the Mecca of pop art, retro furniture and candy style graphics—bringing a breath of fresh air into Walsall. A color of lime green, black and red achieves the pop art look perfectly. White walls teamed up with fluorescent lighted pop station styling units and the lime green Bubble Chairs to complete the look, with colorful pop art images on the walls to reinforce the fun but stylish image. The salon was designed alongside one of the industry's most recognized designers Charlie Hearn who has designed salons for some of the top hairdressers in the country.

Wednesbury has a warm, friendly, relaxed atmosphere and comes with superb shiatsu massage chairs for that all round special pampering. This salon was undergoing a refit in 2011.

salon des saluts

Design Agency: sinato Inc   Client: NATURAL EARTH Inc.   Photography: Toshiyuki Yano

Chikara
Ohno

Architect
Director of sinato Inc.
Part-time lecturer of Kyoto University of Art and Design
1976 Born in Osaka, Japan
1999 Graduated from Department of Civil Engineering, Kanazawa University
2004 Established sinato Inc.

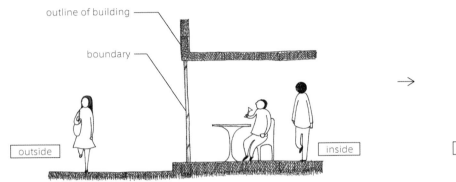

[plane glass]

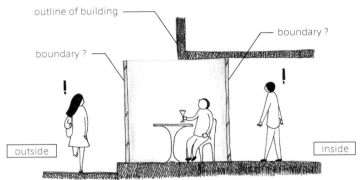

[glass box]

Project Information

The designers designed a small wine bistro fronted on Seijouki Street, Nishiazabu in Tokyo. For the connection between outside street and inside space, considering the value of ambiguous boundary and deep transparency, they decided to crowd 4 small glass boxes into an opening of the building that cross over the outline.

Except one box used for private room inside, other boxes which are used for a court with single olive tree, approach and terrace are outside. It's difficult to know which is a real boundary between inside and outside because this line runs very complicatedly. Besides, every corner of boxes are processed in curves and they bring the visually distortion and blurred transparency to the view from outside.

Another important component, grand plants filled with asparagus, rosemary, ivy, etc. run free curve with floor tile and cross over the glass wall swung as like shore and wave. It emphasizes the ambiguousness of the boundary.

The designers hope what they designed as shop front becomes a kind of public amenity and makes a good experience for not only customer, but for people walking along the street.

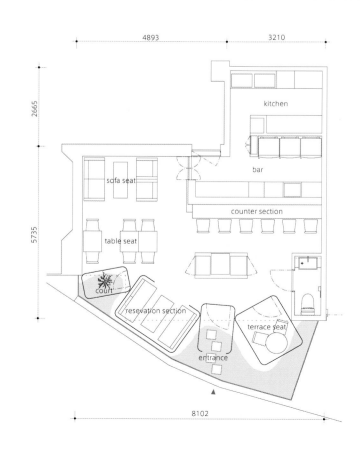

kitchen

bar

counter section

sofa seat

table seat

court

resevation section

terrace seat

entrance

4893

3210

2665

5735

8102

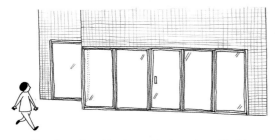

The plane glass skin along with the outline of building.

↓

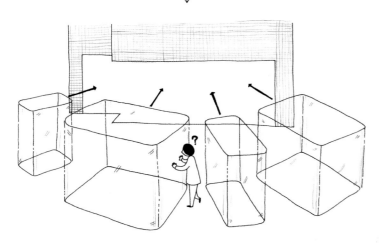

4 glass boxes of which each corner is processed in curve.

↓

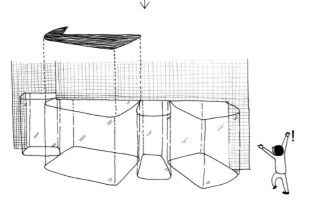

Crowding these boxes into an opening of the building and putting a roof on one box. That is used as inside space.

↓

Plants run free curve, crossing over the glass wall.

salon du fromage

Location: 1st district, Paris, France   Photography: kotaro horiuchi

kotaro horiuchi

2002 diploma of bachelor degree of architecture at university, tokyo
2003 Mecanoo Architecten, Delft
2004 diploma of master degree of architecture and urbanism at graduate school of university, Tokyo
PPAG - Popelka Poduschka Architekten, Vienna
2005 DPA - Dominique Perrault Architecture, Paris
2009 founded office kotaro horiuchi architecture, Paris, Tokyo, Nagoya

A wall with 3 curved surfaces was designed to softly wrap around itself at the center of the space on the ground and 1st floor of the existing building, built during the 18th century.
The surface of the house is a little old, perhaps can let people think of the past.
Inside the house, light yellow light fils the whole space, createing a romantic atmosphere.
The unique droplight attractive people's gaze.
The light shining from "candies", so beautiful.This is really a fashion and sweet design.

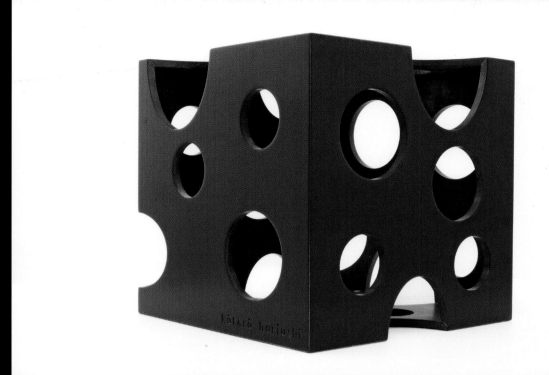

SORA

Design Agency : Keisuke Fujiwara Design Office   Photography: Satoshi Asakawa

Keisuke Fuji-
wara

Keisuke Fujiwara was born in 1968 in Tokyo, Japan. He graduated from the Musashino Art University, and fol-
lowed to work under the renowned interior designer, Shigeru Uchida. After interning at Ron Arad Associates
in 2001, he established Keisuke Fujiwara Design Office which specializes in interior and furniture design. He has
been designing shops for PLEATS PLEASE ISSEY MIYAKE around the world (Japan, France, China, South Korea
and Thailand). Since establishing Keisuke Fujiwara Design Office, his work has been exhibited in the Milan furniture fair, DESIGN MIAMI and INTERIEUR in Kortrijk.

He was awarded first prize from the Japanese Commercial Environment Designer Association.He currently holds
an Associate Professor position at the Tokyo Metropolitan University.

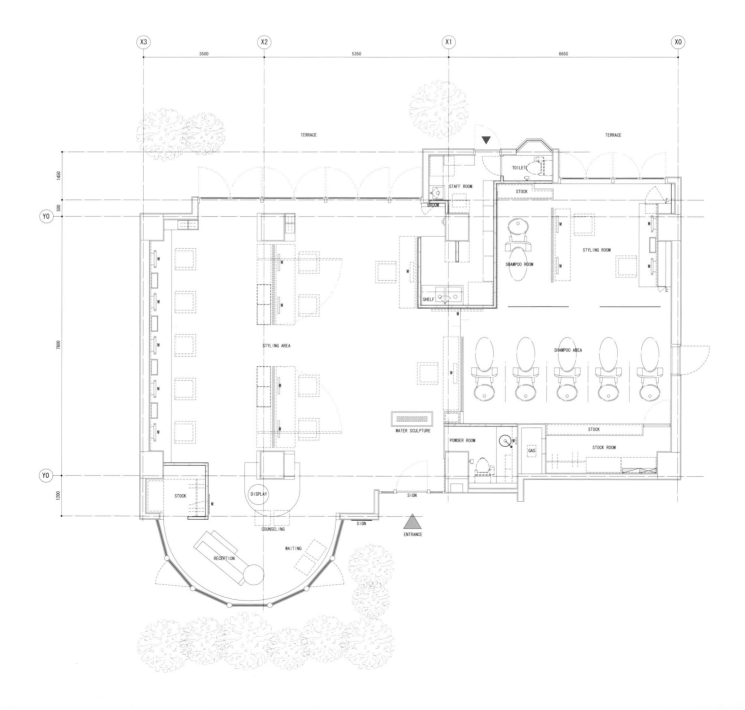

🔷 Project Information

The salon is mainly consists of 12 different timber. The color of the timber gives a gradation in the salon as if the sky changes its color in one day. This is one of the most important symbolic elements in SORA. Sky changes everyday and moment, season to season, sunshine to rain, cloud to snow. It has countless effectiveness. To create SORA "the sky" light and water plays an important part within this salon. The designer hopes the salon connects with "space","time" and "people" like SORA who connects all.

Entrance, Water Feature
The water feature welcome customers at the entrance. The ripples and dripping sound from the slow water drops, created a relaxing atmosphere while waiting to be seated. The drop also gives a spark of light, which makes the water feature looks stunning and elegant.

Mirrors
The mirrors have the same size as "Mona Lisa" painting, painted by Leonardo Da Vinci. The idea is to give customers the beauty of Mona Lisa.

Shampoo Area
The designer did not use any pendent or spot light at the shampoo space, to avoid glare while lying on the comfortable shampoo sofa.

Styling Space
The two panels constructed by many vertical timber beams at the centre of the styling spaces, can be rotated 90 degrees. It gives a dynamic variety and fresh look in the salon, depends on season and mood.

Private Styling Space
The partition of the vertical timber beams consists of 12 different woods. They are randomly placed and form the letter S, O, R, and A which can be recognized through the mirrors.

Existing Parts
The wooden flooring and steel sash have been part of the existing building for 20 years. The designer decided to keep them as they are.

Lighting Design
LED lighting is settled in the terrace. It provides a rainbow colors and adjustable with time, seasons or events.

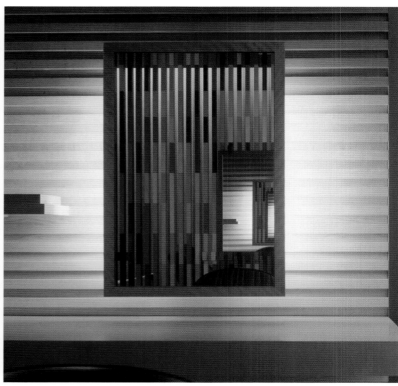

Lodge

Location: Hiroshima, Japan   Design Agency : Suppose Design Office

Suppose

Makoto Tanijiri was born in 1974. In 2000 he started Suppose Design Office, an architectural design firm in Hiroshima. His work covers a broad range of areas including designing houses, business spaces, site frameworks, landscapes, products, and art installations. For the projects, he collaborated with structural engineers such as Ono Japan and Nawaken Jimu. In 2008, he started 2nd office in Tokyo, and since the time, he has been promoting many projects both in Japan and overseas. He completed an installation project of TOSHIBA LED light at Milano Salone 2010. He has got a lot of awards and other achievements, such as the JCD Rookie Award, the Heiwa-ohashi Pedestrian Bridge Design Proposal Competition as a finalist. He is also a part time professor of Anabuki Design College.

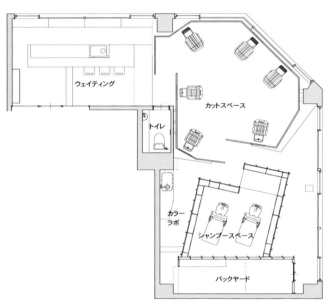

平面図s=1/150

The hair salon offers two spaces, one is close and the other is open, to meet demands both of customers and workers. The place is divided in three spaces with a mirror and shelves, and there are no walls just as dividers. The mirror is floating and placed only at the customers' eyelevel, and it also works as a long continuous partition for the middle of space.

Because of the mirror and shelves, views of all customers who are sitting on a chair, are blocked, and they could feel the space more private. On the other hand, workers could have a view for the whole space over the top of the dividers. To control the height of the partitions made the hair salon possible to have the two types of spaces for both of customers and staff who have opposite demands to a salon space. Moreover, the mirror stainless plate also function to create a flow of the space, and the surface combined mirror and vibration finish could emphasize the movement more.

To delete all stereotypes of hair salon, and think about each interactive relationship at the space, was a

chance to notice more possibilities of creating the salon. Makoto Tanijiri believes to design a base of ideas is more important than to design the actual space, and the process has more potential to create new space yet keeping the original function.

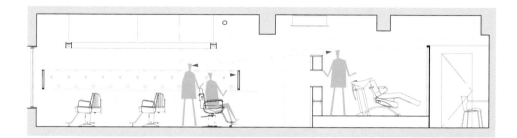

Soan hair

Location: Hiroshima, Japan   Design Agency : Suppose Design Office

Suppose   Makoto Tanijiri was born in 1974. In 2000 he started Suppose Design Office, an architectural design firm in Hiroshima. His work covers a broad range of areas including designing houses, business spaces, site frameworks, landscapes, products, and art installations. For the projects, he collaborated with structural engineers such as Ono Japan and Nawaken Jimu. In 2008, he started 2nd office in Tokyo, and since the time, he has been promoting many projects both in Japan and overseas. He completed an installation project of TOSHIBA LED light at Milano Salone 2010. He has got a lot of awards and other achievements, such as the JCD Rookie Award, the Heiwa-ohashi Pedestrian Bridge Design Proposal Competition as a finalist. He is also a part time professor of Anabuki Design College.

This is a hair salon project that was considered how to divide a place as it was also formed in a continuous space, like a forest that is separated by trees but also continued with trees. Wall thickness was considered carefully for the small store, which has 46 m² and should have three areas, cutting, washing and waiting space. 24mm plywood was used for partitions of the three places. The walls could offer proper floor space and circulation for each section. The separations are shaped as trees. They are designed to continue like panels that are strong and easy to build. The tree partitions are layered in the store. At the point they are crossed each other, the panels are shaped as 3 dimensional trees, and the simple combination of 2D and 3D partitions create complex view in the salon. The partitions were layered, however the view never blocked but continue through the gaps between the branches-shaped plywood such as trees in a forest. Moreover, the tree framed partitions, which is suppose to be an architectural elements, could also described identity of the store as a salon to offer customers comfortable space and time. The iconic tree is also used for a facade of the building, and it would create welcome atmosphere to the sidewalk in front of the building with the tree-icons that is continuing to the inside.

TYM

Location: Nnagano , Japan   Design Agency : no.555 (number fives architectural design office)

no.555

no.555 is an architecture design office located in center of Yokohama-city, Kanagawa prefecture, Japan owned by architect Takuya Tsuchida. Takuya Tsuchida, whose father is also an architect, was born in Fukushima-prefecture in 1973. When designing the furniture, architecture, and the city, and people's minds and the movement of people and more interested in design. That is because he believe the most beautiful shape. He is trying to offer better directionality and a new sense from existing life and the idea. And buildings change and grow with and by users. The most im-

portant concept is selected in all the project in order to share the same direction with the clients. The shape shall be created purely from the concept by making full use of latest and traditional technology.

Project Information

The site is located in a business district where unplaned land lines up in the heartland of Nagano Prefecture. In the near future, high-rise construction lines is planed to the vicinity, and a lively 32m wide road of is planned as for the frontal road.

The house with the hair salon was planned here. First of all, walls were planned around the site to guard the site from the neighbor and maintain. The functional big is inserted deeply in the 3rd and 4th floor to secure the lighting and ventilation. Interior partitions are maintained to waist height in order to show the exterior view of exterior wall slit from anywhere. The hair salon is located on the second floor. Since the salon is targeted to the middle-age, the building looks sealed to give the brand image "the customer is covered and secure". The building is designed to secure residential comfort and salon brand at same time to endure the surrounding change in the future.

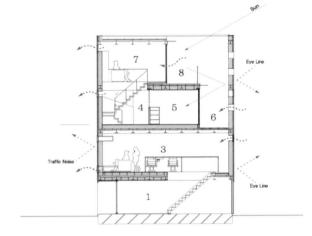

1. Hair Salon Entrance
2. Staff room
3. Hair Salon
4. Corridor
5. Bed room
6. Terrace A
7. Livingroom
8. Terrace B

Section

1. Garage
2. Salon Entrance
3. Staff room
4. Machine room
5. House Entrance

1F Floor Plan

1. Waiting room
2. Counter
3. Shampoo Space
4. Cut Space

2F Floor Plan

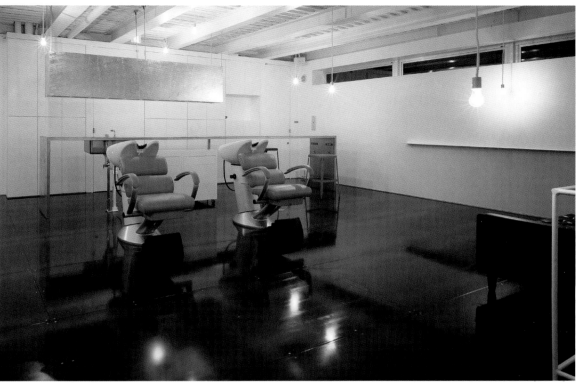

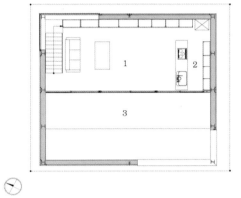

1. Residential Hall
2. Corridor
3. Powder room
4. Bath room
5. Bed room 1
6. Bed room 2
7. Bed room 3
8. Terrace A

3F Floor Plan

1. Living room
2. KItchen
3. Terrace B

4F Floor Plan

Xantippe

Design Agency : Lieven Musschoot   Client: Christine by Xantippe   Photography: Thomas De Bruyne

Lieven Musschoot

Year of Birth: 1968
Country: Belgium
Company name / label: LMMH
Also known for: His interior works for Pure C and other tasty projects
Also works for: Sywawa, Wevre & Ducré
Interesting to know: Works together with Mathias,
you don't know where one man's inspiration
ends and the other's creativity starts.

Project Information

Inspiration: Zen,space,light,and the ultimate event.

Materials: ceiling uses gold and white stretch ceiling, floor uses white epoxy with shredded paper and dark oak parquet, walls use gold wall ceilings and white steel.

The sandstone is the main theme of the design. The design adopts flow chair by MDF Italia and tables in white steel by Lieven Musschoot. Delta light-Led Lighting is custom made by Tronixx Belgium, and poxy-wever & Ducré was used for wall lighting.

The design concept is to create a salon that does not look like a hair salon. There is a perfect balans between work area(white space) and waiting-lounging (golden space). The design wants to create a loft feeling.Bringing together of materials,everything must be right to the last details.

Customers feel relaxed in this hair salon. Functionality is very important. The space is 300 m² in all.

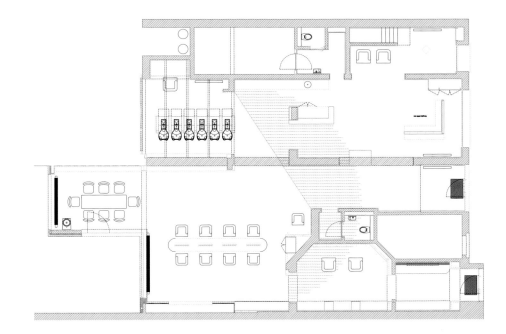

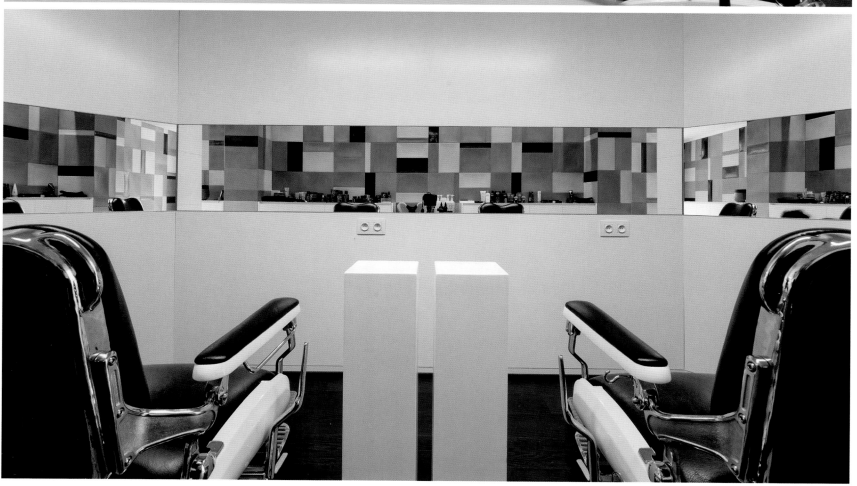

Tiffany modelling design

Location: Jiangsu, China   Design Agency : Kunshan Xunping Design, Decoration & Engineering Co. , Ltd.   Area: 256m²

Jonny

Jonny is graduated from the Art School in Xiamen in 1996, and he is the general manager and design director of Kunshan Xunping Design, Decoration & Engineering Co. , Ltd. His works were published in many books. He is also a member of China Interior Design Association.

His design style is diversification, innovation, satisfying the customer requirements with the greatest efforts.

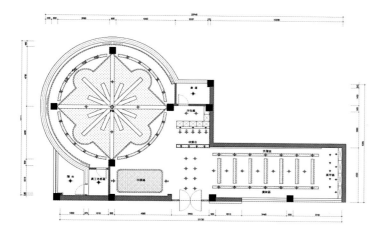

"Tiffany modelling design" is located in the largest shopping paradise of Taicang, NanYang square. "Tiffany" not only need to satisfy the modern aesthetic requirements, but also need to the spirit of the salon.

Based on the basic concept of trend and fashion, "tiffany" shop based on square. The ground is consist of different specifications of black and white square which form a gradual change.

The design focus on the choice of materials, and the collocation of color, so that it is more popular, more fashion and more outstanding.

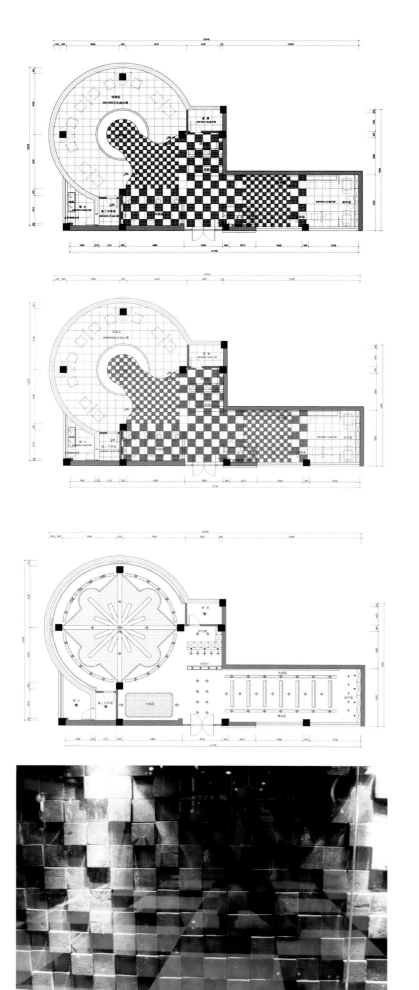

Xupin & Impression
Cosmetology and Hair Dressing

Location: Jiangsu, China   Design Agency : Kunshan Xunping Design, Decoration & Engineering Co. , Ltd.   Area: 510m²

Jonny   Jonny is graduated from the Art School in XiaMen in 1996, and he is the general manager and design director of Kunshan Xunping Design, Decoration & Engineering Co. , Ltd. His works were published in many books. He is also a member of China Interior Design Association.

His design style is diversification, innovation, satisfying the customer requirements with the greatest efforts.

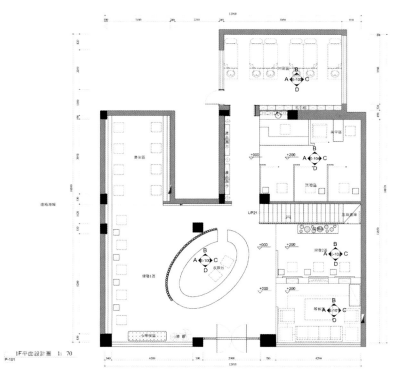

Nowadays, the design of hair salon is becoming more and more popular and avant-garde. This salon is the mix and match of fashion and nature in its design.

As popular as others, the cashier desk and hair dressing areas are impressive: arc-shaped cashier desk is eye-catching in the light of sparkling mosaic ceiling; both rows of chairs in the hairdressing area are placed symmetrically, while the whole room looks more transparent and lightful as the mirrors reflecting the light.

The salon is also decorated with a lot of green plants and a path of cobblestones. Hairdressing here, is not merely a simple shaving, but even a pleasing experience.

The whole planning of space is fulfilled with estheticism. In the lights of both blue and silvery, this estheticism is cultivated to its maximum: the whole space becomes suffused with an amazing air of mystery and romance.

2F平面設計圖 1: 70
P-101

SV hair salon in Shenzhen Aihua

An fujian

Social Position: member of China Architecture Interior Design Institution
Graduate School: Qiqihar university

Study and Work Experience:
Desginer of Beijing Yuanzhou Adornment Co., LTD
and Shenzhen Shenzhuang Adornment Industry Co., LTD.
Partners of Shenzhen Yashang Design Co., LTD

The designer has no more confidence at the beginning of drawing the sketch, for the PVC pipes have been used as the carrier of wire protection. Most people pay more attention to the materials themselves, but the designer thinks that the materials have more meanings than themselves. The materials are full of nature beauty and language, only people who touch the real materials could further understand of them, so as to explore the kinds of hiding possibilities .

The designer tries to develop a kind of characteristic or change a type of characteristic. The visual experience is usually brought by changing the materials. To understand the "changeable" of material benefits to build the "motion cognition" between people and materials.

SV hair salon in Shenzhen Caitian

An fujian

Social Position: member of China Architecture Interior Design Institution
Graduate School: Qiqihar university

Study and Work Experience:
Desginer of Beijing Yuanzhou Adornment Co., LTD
and Shenzhen Shenzhuang Adornment Industry Co., LTD.
Partners of Shenzhen Yashang Design Co., LTD

The elegance is unforgettable after being tired of seeing a wave of noise and vanity. Obviously, elegance is by no means of an apparent thing, but needs the fashion wisdom with care and precise of sculpting as well as withstands the precipitate of style taste. Upon receiving this case and listening the customer's request, it bring pressure to the designer which not only has to meet the customer's needs but also to understand the adaption of new environment. After being completed, this case meets the expectable results. The sense of noble and elegant wins all the applause.

Salon GIL LERICHE

Location: 110 centre commercial St Sever, ROUEN, France   Architect : Linda HENRY

GAMMA &amp GAMMA &amp officially born 30 years ago. The design team makes an expert fusion of design and production techniques, together with the historical knowledge of the profession with its own specific needs. Quality of construction as well as salon image are the key elements upon which GAMMA &amp and BROSS SPA focuses its entrepreneurial commitment. Now the company sells its upscale furniture in more than 50 countries and the distribution network has been developed in more than 30 countries.

 **Project Information**

This design's mass-tone is purple. It is a elegant hair salon, but brings a feeling of relaxing, The neat modelling chair and lamps are very contemporary. The combination of ceiling design and the ground is so perfect that people can feel a romantic and sweet world.

Salon Olivier Delmulle

Location: 258 rue Failherbe, WATERLOOS, France   Architect : Linda HENRY

GAMMA &amp   GAMMA &amp officially born 30 years ago. The design team makes an expert fusion of design and production techniques, together with the historical knowledge of the profession with its own specific needs. Quality of construction as well as salon image are the key elements upon which GAMMA &amp and BROSS SPA focuses its entrepreneurial commitment. Now the company sells its upscale furniture in more than 50 countries and the distribution network has been developed in more than 30 countries.

 Project Information

The appropriate combination of black and white, the simple colors and the pleasant light help people relax down. This is a nice place for peace and quietness, those who have a whole day's busy work would take a break here: the washed/cut hair bring away all their fatigue. Watched from the outside, this salon shapes a corridor. As you go deeper, the checkout, hairdressing, resting and washing areas come into your eyes accordingly, whispering that they are always there to serve you.

Fashion Point
Location: Italy   Designer : Linda HENRY

GAMMA &amp GAMMA &amp officially born 30 years ago. The design team makes an expert fusion of design and production techniques, together with the historical knowledge of the profession with its own specific needs. Quality of construction as well as salon image are the key elements upon which GAMMA &amp and BROSS SPA focuses its entrepreneurial commitment. Now the company sells its upscale furniture in more than 50 countries and the distribution network has been developed in more than 30 countries.

Hasselt

GAMMA &amp GAMMA &amp officially born 30 years ago. The design team makes an expert fusion of design and production techniques, together with the historical knowledge of the profession with its own specific needs. Quality of construction as well as salon image are the key elements upon which GAMMA &amp and BROSS SPA focuses its entrepreneurial commitment. Now the company sells its upscale furniture in more than 50 countries and the distribution network has been developed in more than 30 countries.

Cudmore & Co Hair & Beauty Spa

Design Agency: Fahrenheit Design Ltd   Client: Mark Cudmore – Cudmore & Co   Photography: Andy Kruczek Photography

Kevin Keane

Fahrenheit Design Ltd are a multi-disciplined design consultancy based in Coventry, UK. As specialists in retail and leisure design, Fahrenheit has designed over 200 salons & spas for a wide range of clients. Always looking for something new, Fahrenheit merge leisure concepts in to retail design installations to create a unique blend of ideas.

Fahrenheit Design Ltd offer the following: conceptual design, 2D & 3D visualization, specification, sourcing products, design co-ordination, project management, installation and handover amongst other services.

Project Information

Cudmore & Co is a dynamic, vibrant and atmospheric hair and beauty salon situated in affluent Solihull, UK. The brief was to create an environment which stood apart from other salon designs and challenge the best salon interiors. A striking design of curved walls, varying levels of ceiling, 3 metre frosted glass panels, color changing lights and dominant red features throughout add to the dramatic effect. The centre piece of the interior is the entrance area which is designed with a fire rated stretch ceiling inset with light-fittings that circle over the glass and Corian reception counter. A Champagne bar and private consultation area run alongside the dedicated ladies area boasting massaging backwashes with a hot towel warmers.

The "Gents" area provides a unique experience with boys toys in the independent waiting area. Barbering, traditional cut throat shaving, a bottle bar and an Aqua Vibra automatic hair-washer are available, which sprays water and shampoo onto the head whilst the client reclines. 8 individually designed beauty rooms, a training academy and offices make up the first floor of this exquisite salon & spa.

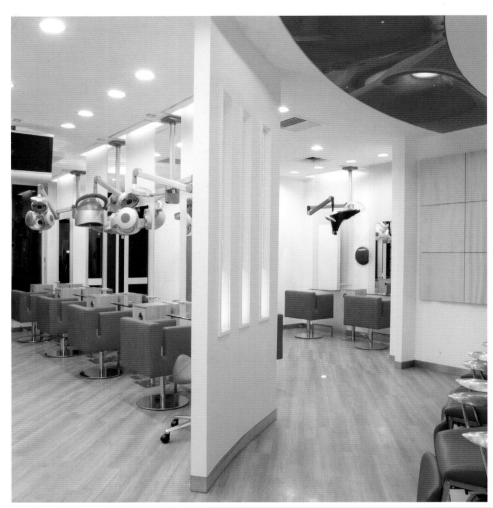

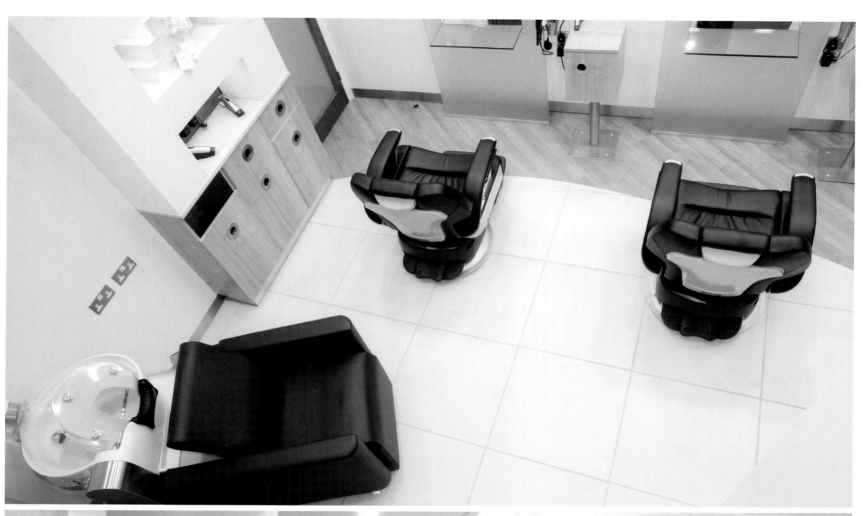

ARTPOWER

Acknowledgement
We would like to thank all the designers and companies who made significant contributions to the compilation of this book. Without them, this project would not have been possible. We would also like to thank many others whose names did not appear on the credits, but made specific input and support for the project from beginning to end.

Future Editions
If you would like to contribute to the next edition of Artpower, please email us
your details to: info@artpower.com.cn.

Artpower International Publishing Co., Ltd.

As medium of delivering the Power of Art, with all its cooperative art creators, Artpower has been working on the publication and distribution of books under the tenet of "vitalizing business through art" since its establishment in areas of "Advertising Creativity, Brand Identity, Packaging Display and Photography". During its developing history, the company has provided global readers with numerous excellent books on advertising, design, marketing and media, by means of shop selling, in–city free delivery, mail order and online sales. It is also a growing agency for some fine professional magazines.

 Main Businesses

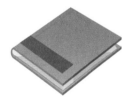

Copyrighted Books   Authorized Books   Business Portfolios & Brochures

WE WORK ON AN AREA WHERE ART MARRIES TECHNOLOGY;

WE ARE A TEAM DEVELOPING WITH ALL OUR PARTNERS;

WE HAVE CREATIVE THINKING AND PROVIDE QUALITY SERVICE.

Address: 21/F, Skyline Commercial Center,
71–77 Wing Lok Street, SheungWan,
Tel: 852 3184 0676
Fax: 852 2543 2396
URL: www.artpower.com.cn
E–mail: artpower@artpower.com.cn

ARTPOWER

 2012 New Arrivals

 **STORES**
978-988-19735-9-7
245 X 300 mm
232 Pages(vol.1)
240 Pages(vol.2)
Hardback
August 2011

 **THE WORLD SPA DESIGN**
978-988-19735-8-0
245 X 290 mm
248 Pages(vol.1)
264 Pages(vol.2)
Hardback
September 2011

 **WAY OF THE SIGN II**
978-988-19735-6-6
210 X 290 mm
280 Pages
Hardback
October 2011

 **PAPER ART**
978-988-15742-0-6
210 X 270 mm
488 Pages
Hardback
November 2011

 **NEW TYPOGRAPHY**
978-988-15742-8-2
210 X 270mm
Hardback
280 Pages
English

 **Hong Zhongxuan's 359°**
-a photography collection of
design elements
978-7-5611-6613-0
230 X 300 mm
Hardback
360 Pages
English

 **Sales Promotion Design**
978-4-568-50455-2
225 X 297 mm
Hardback
288 Pages
English/Japanese

 **Design Feast**
978-988-68578-2-3
220 X 290 mm
288 Pages
Hardback
May 2011

 **Design Art of Villa**
978-988-15743-1-2
245 X 290 mm
Hardback
352 Pages
English

 **TOP VILLAS
OF INTERNATIONAL STYLE**
978-988-15743-9-8
310 X 450 mm
Hardback
480 Pages
English

 **Office Design**
978-988-18893-8-6
240 X 295 mm
488 Pages
Hardback
February 2011

 **Public Construction**
978-988-15742-2-0
247 X 330 mm
Hardback
416 Pages
English/Japanese

 **Restaurant and Bar Design II**
978-7-5611-5860-9
245 X 300 mm
Hardback
344 Pages
English

 **Dessert Station**
978-988-15743-2-9
245 X 290 mm
Hardback
360 Pages
English

 **Office Design**
978-988-19748-6-8
245 X 290 mm
Hardback
392 Pages
English